365 DESIGNS

cross stitch all through the year

by Sam Hawkins

American School of Needlework®, Inc., San Marcos, California

Bobbie Matela, Managing Editor
Carol Wilson Mansfield, Art Director
Jane Cannon Meyers, Creative Director
Ann Harnden, Editor
Pam Nichols, Editorial Assistant
Mary Hernandez, Book Design

Cross stitch charts by Debbie Andersen, Pat Hawes,
Betsy Meyers Knight, Cheri Lowry, and Brent Rathburn

Photographed designs were stitched by: Kellie Ault,
Donna Bachman, Penny Boswinkle, Jill Brooks,
Lucile Carlson, Lynda Carlson, Linda Causee,
Barbara Chancy, Stephanie Cook, Debbie Davis,
Maryann Donovan, Ellen Harnden, Lisa Hebb, Pat Hicks,
Betsy Knight, Janet Kazmer, Marsha Landry,
Maxine Meadows, Margaret Minor, Pam Nichols,
Janice Orantes, Mary Alice Patsko, Petie Pickwick,
Carly Poggemeyer, Carrie Snider, Lee Ann Tibbals,
Kathy Tregembo, Jacquetta Vogel, Jody West,
Julie Williams, Nancy Withrow, and Connie Wright.

Contents

	page(s)
Introduction	3
Cross Stitch Basics	4-7
Design Index by Subject	8
Spring	
Color Photos	9-12
Design Directory	13
Charts	14-44
Summer	
Color Photos	45-48
Design Directory	49
Charts	50-80
Autumn	
Color Photos	81-84
Design Directory	85
Charts	86-116
Winter	
Color Photos	117-120
Design Directory	121
Charts	122-152

**Refer to the Design Directory for each season to find the number and
location of the charted designs.**

Front Cover　　　**Back Cover**

Metric Measures
(approximate conversions)
1 inch = 2.5cm
5 inches = 12.7cm
10 inches = 25.4cm

Introduction

Sam Hawkins is a name familiar to every cross stitch addict. Sam's designs have appeared in dozens of books, magazines and kits, bringing many happy hours of stitching to cross stitchers throughout the world.

This book showcases 365 delightful Sam Hawkins designs—enough so that you can stitch a different design every day for a year!

The first embroidery most children learn is cross stitch, working little Xs on towels or pillowcases stamped with the design. Today's counted cross stitch has come a long way from that humble beginning. Cross stitch now is a sophisticated art that appeals to all ages.

In fact, counted cross stitch is the most widely done form of embroidery. Instead of working our stitches over stamped Xs, we work elaborate designs on blank, evenweave fabric, following a printed chart. The results are spectacular, though the actual stitching is quick, easy and fun.

Sam Hawkins' special touch adds incredible detail to small designs. This book is divided into seasonal chapters, but the designs are versatile enough that most can be used throughout the year. In addition to their seasonal aspects, we've given you an index by design subject on page 8, making it easy to find just the motif you are looking for.

Sam is a fine arts graduate of Ohio State University, and has designed in many areas of needlework. When not at his drawing board, Sam is an avid gardener and was appointed to the Arts Commission of the City of Oceanside, California.

Jean Leinhauser

Jean Leinhauser, President
American School of Needlework®

Cross Stitch Basics

Materials

The materials required for counted cross stitch are few and inexpensive: a piece of evenweave fabric, a tapestry needle, some 6-strand cotton floss, scissors, and a charted design. An embroidery hoop is optional. All of these are readily available at most needlework shops.

Fabrics

For counted cross stitch embroidery we use "evenweave" fabrics which are woven with the same number of horizontal and vertical threads per inch. Cross stitches are made over the intersections of the horizontal and vertical threads, and because the number of threads in each direction is equal, each stitch will be the same size and perfectly square. A fabric is described by the number of threads (or groups of threads) per inch; the number is called its thread count.

A counted cross stitch design can be worked on any count of fabric you choose, but that thread count will determine the finished size of the stitched design. A higher thread count will produce a smaller design (more stitches are worked per inch) and a lower thread count will produce a larger design because there are fewer stitches per inch.

Evenweave fabrics commonly used for cross stitch are Aida cloth, linen, and an array of specialty fabrics. There are also many kinds of pre-made evenweave products.

Aida cloth is a cotton that has groups of four threads woven in a basketweave pattern, making the intersections very easy to see when constructing stitches. The groups of threads are called squares. Aida is woven in several different sizes, measured by the number of squares (therefore stitches) per inch: 11-count (11 stitches to the inch), 14-count (14 stitches to the inch), 16-count (16 stitches to the inch), and 18-count (18 stitches to the inch).

Figs 1 to **4** show a simple tulip border, cross-stitched on the four sizes of Aida. The more stitches to the inch, the smaller the design will be. Thus a design stitched on 18-count fabric will be considerably smaller than one stitched on 11-count fabric.

11-count

Fig 1

14-count

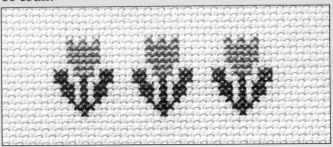

Fig 2

16-count

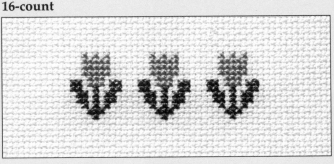

Fig 3

18-count

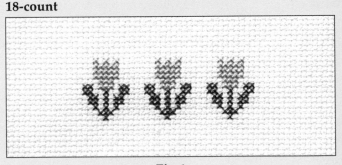

Fig 4

Remember...

The number of stitches per inch made on any evenweave fabric determines the size of a design after it's worked.

Linen is woven of single round linen threads. Cross stitches are made over two threads in each direction. Linen may be a bit difficult for beginners to use as there are no obvious intersections as on Aida, but a little practice will produce great results.

Linen is available in a variety of thread counts. Because stitches are worked over two threads, the number of stitches per inch will be half the thread count. For example, on 28-count linen, you will work 14 stitches per inch—or the same finished size as if the designs were worked on 14-count Aida cloth.

Specialty Fabrics are woven in the same manner as linen, but may be cotton, linen, synthetic, or a combination of fibers. They have different thread counts and may be known by different names, depending on the manufacturer.

There are also some non-fabric surfaces that are popular for counted cross stitch; the following are all 14-count materials. Vinyl-Weave™ is a vinyl product that looks like Aida cloth, is impervious to water, and does not ravel. Perforated paper is a pressed paper with small round holes (perforations) and stitches are made over the spaces between perforations; it is somewhat fragile. Perforated plastic is a plastic canvas that looks like perforated paper and is structurally stronger than the paper.

Should you wish to cross stitch on a non-evenweave surface, you can use waste canvas, a temporary evenweave product that is available in a variety of thread counts. Baste a piece of canvas onto the surface to be embroidered, work over the canvas threads, then remove them when stitching is complete.

Pre-made Products are wonderful if you want to cross stitch a fingertip towel, a pillow, or perhaps a baby bib, but you don't like to sew. You'll love the many pre-mades available with an evenweave fabric (usually Aida) part of the construction. In addition to those we've mentioned, you'll find table linens, kitchen and bath accessories, afghans, bookmarks, a variety of baby items, and many others.

Needles

A small blunt-tipped tapestry needle, size 24 or 26, will be used for stitching. The higher the needle number, the smaller the needle. The correct size needle is easy to thread with the amount of thread required, but is not so large that it will distort the holes in the fabric. Threaded, the needle should easily slip through the fabric. **Fig 5** will tell you which size needle is appropriate for each kind of fabric.

Fabric	Stitches Per Inch	Strands of Floss	Tapestry Needle Size
Aida	11	3	22 or 24
Aida	14	2	24 or 26
Aida	16	2	24 or 26
Aida	18	1 or 2	26

Fig 5

Have a good supply of needles on hand. When working with several colors, thread several needles in advance, so they are ready when you want to change colors.

Threads

The commonly used thread for counted cross stitch is six-strand cotton embroidery floss. It can be divided to work with one, two, or more strands at a time. Our cover and color pages were stitched with Anchor embroidery floss, but we also give the identifying color numbers for DMC in a color key with every design. Both companies have their own color range, so these suggestions are not perfect color matches, but work within the specific design.

Generic color names are given for each floss color in a design; for example, if there is only one green it will be so named, but if there are three greens, they will be labeled lt (light), med (medium), and dk (dark). The name of the floss color is not important—it is only for reference when looking at an array of floss colors. Match each symbol to the number of your chosen brand of floss.

Separate floss into individual strands, then put the required number back together before threading the needle. **Fig 5** tells how many floss strands to use with different thread counts of fabric. Two strands of floss are usually used to cross stitch on a 14-count background. The surface will be adequately covered by the stitches, yet the delicacy of the pattern is retained. For a more solid color effect, use two strands of floss on 16-count Aida as shown on the covers and color pages in this book.

A more delicate value of a color may be achieved by stitching on 14- or 16-count fabric with only one strand of floss as in Design 331 on page 139. Or, if you choose to work one of these designs on a very dark fabric, you may wish to add a third strand of floss when stitching with light colors so the background is thoroughly covered.

Blending filament is used to add some sparkle to an area of a design. Thread your needle with the desired floss, then thread a strand of filament and stitch with the three strands. Occasionally you will be directed to use one strand each of floss and filament. Metallic gold thread is also used to add a festive touch to a design. We chose Kreinik® #8 (fine) braid, using a single strand for cross stitching and backstitching. If desired, metallic thread can be used instead of the braid; work with the appropriate number of strands of your chosen brand.

Hoops

The use of a hoop or frame to hold your stitching is optional, but it will depend on personal preference and/or choice of fabric. If you are more comfortable with a hoop, choose a clean plastic or wood version with a screw-type tension adjuster. Be sure to remove the hoop when you are not stitching, and avoid crushing stitched areas as you progress.

Scissors

A pair of small, sharp-pointed scissors is necessary, especially for snipping misplaced stitches. You may want to hang your scissors on a chain or ribbon around your neck—you'll need them often.

Charted Designs

Counted cross stitch designs are worked from charts. Each square on a chart represents the space for one cross stitch. Each chart is accompanied by a color key, which gives the numbers of the suggested floss colors; a symbol in a square represents the floss color to be used for the cross stitch. Directions for placement of the following decorative stitches are also given. Straight lines over or between symbols indicate backstitches or straight stitches and a dashed line designates running stitch. Lazy daisies are shown by their shape and French knots usually by dots.

If a color name appears without a preceding symbol and equal sign, the color is only used for a decorative stitch. The stitch width and height are given for each design, and arrows indicate the centers vertically and horizontally. Occasionally a design will be a repeat pattern, so we indicate the beginning and ending of a repeat section with a bar and arrows rather than one center arrow.

Charts can be foolers: The size of the charted design is not necessarily the size that your finished work will be. The worked size is determined by the number of threads per inch of the fabric you select. For example, whenever you work a motif that is 22 stitches wide and 11 stitches high on 11-count Aida, the worked design will be 2" wide and 1" high. Worked on 18-count Aida the same design will be 1 1/4" wide and about 1/2" high. Use the chart below, **Fig 6**, as a guide to determine the finished width and height of a stitched design based on your chosen background fabric.

Thread Count	Number of Stitches in Design				
	10	20	30	40	50
11-count	1"	1 ¾"	2 ¾"	3 ⅝"	4 ½"
14-count	¾"	1 ⅜"	2 ⅛"	2 ⅞"	3 ⅝"
16-count	⅝"	1 ¼"	1 ⅞"	2 ½"	3 ⅛"
18-count	½"	1 ⅛"	1 ⅝"	2 ¼"	2 ¾"
(measurements are given to the nearest ⅛")					

Fig 6

Getting Started

Follow the arrows to find the center of a charted design; count threads or fold fabric to find its center. Count up and over to the left on chart and fabric to begin cross stitching.

Cut floss into comfortable working lengths—we suggest about 18". To begin, bring threaded needle to front of fabric. Hold an inch of the end against the back, then anchor it with your first few stitches. To end threads and begin new ones next to existing stitches, weave through the backs of several stitches. Trim thread ends close to fabric. Wherever possible, end your thread under stitches of the same color.

If you are a beginning stitcher, we suggest you work the tulip design shown as a border in **Figs 1** to **4** on page 4 .

Fig 7 shows the chart and color key for one tulip motif. If needed, refer to The Stitches below.

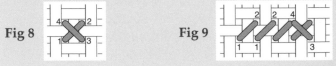

Fig 7

Tulip Motif
Design size: 9 wide x 12 high

		Anchor	DMC
♥	= pink	75	962
+	= green	244	702

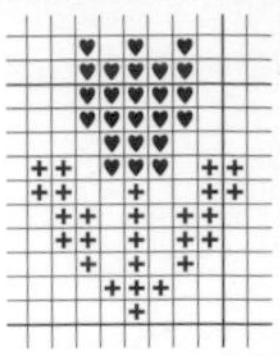

Thread two needles, one with pink and one with green floss. Using pink floss, work the tulip portion of the design shown by the heart symbol. Begin with the three stitches across the top: Work half of each stitch from left to right, skipping the in-between squares, then complete the stitches on the return. Work the remaining five horizontal rows. End off thread. Using green floss, work the leaves and the stem portion of the design, shown by the plus symbol, in the same manner. To create a border, repeat for each tulip, but do not carry floss from one tulip to the next.

The Stitches

Note: Unless otherwise noted in the individual color key, use two strands of floss for cross stitches, French knots, lazy daisies, running stitches, and straight stitches; use one strand for backstitches.

Cross Stitch

The basic cross stitch is formed in two steps. **Fig 8** shows how to make a single cross stitch on Aida cloth. Follow the numbering and bring needle up at 1, down at 2, up at 3, and down at 4 to complete the stitch. Whenever possible, work horizontal rows of stitches, **Fig 9**. Work half of each stitch (1-2) across the row from left to right; on the return journey from right to left, complete each stitch with the 3-4 sequence.

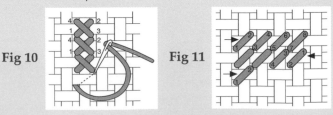

Fig 8   **Fig 9**

When a vertical row of stitches is appropriate for the design, complete each stitch then proceed to the next, **Fig 10**. No matter how you work the stitches, make sure that all crosses slant in the same direction.

The effect of a floss color may be softened by working half cross stitches, **Fig 11**. Work only the first half of each cross stitch. Because you do not return to your starting point at the left side, we suggest you work left-to-right rows in the usual manner, from the bottom to the top of the stitch. On the return right-to-left row, you can work a similar slope from the top to the bottom of the stitch. Work row three as for row one, etc.

Fig 10   **Fig 11**

Backstitch

Backstitches are worked after cross stitches have been completed. They may slope in any direction and are occasionally worked over more than one square of fabric. **Fig 12** shows the progression of several stitches; bring thread up at odd numbers and down at even numbers.

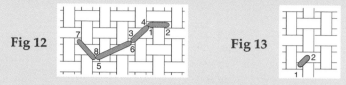

Fig 12 **Fig 13**

Occasionally a very short backstitched line is required for a design, **Fig 13**. It will appear on the chart as a line that occupies less than a square, so you will make a partial backstitch of the length and direction shown on the chart. If a thicker backstitch is required, the color key will note the use of two strands (2 strands) rather than the usual one strand for that part of the design.

Sometimes you have to choose where to end one backstitch color and begin the next color. As a rule of thumb, choose the object that should appear closest to you. Backstitch around that shape with the appropriate color, then backstitch the areas behind it with adjacent color(s).

Straight Stitch

A straight stitch, **Fig 14**, is made like a long backstitch. Come up at one end of the stitch and down at the other. Be sure to secure thread well at the beginning and ending of a group of straight stitches so they stay taut.

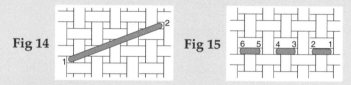

Fig 14 **Fig 15**

Running Stitch

This stitch resembles basting. Bring thread up at odd numbers and down at even numbers, **Fig 15**. Follow position and direction shown on chart.

French Knot

Bring thread up where indicated on chart. Wrap floss once around needle, and reinsert needle close to, but at least one thread away, from where thread first came up, **Figs 16, 17,** and **18**. Hold wrapping thread tightly, close to surface of fabric. Pull needle through, letting thread go just as knot is formed. For a larger knot, use more strands of floss, but wrap only once. **Fig 16** shows a French knot in the middle of a vacant square of Aida, **Fig 17** shows one at the corner of a square, and **Fig 18** shows one on top of a cross stitch.

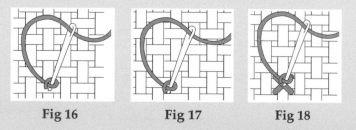

Fig 16 **Fig 17** **Fig 18**

Lazy Daisy Stitch

This stitch creates pointed oval shapes that resemble flower petals. Bring thread up at center hole (1), **Fig 19**. Loop floss, insert needle in same hole, and bring it out two squares from center (2) or as indicated on chart, with loop beneath point of needle. Pull needle through, adjusting size and shape of loop. Stitch down over loop, one thread farther from center, to secure it. Repeat for each oval shape. Anchor ending thread especially well on the wrong side.

Fig 19

Planning A Project

We have shown these 365 designs worked in graphic arrangements by season. You can work any of the designs alone as a small project, two or three as companion pieces, or you can combine similar designs to cover a larger surface. However you choose to use the designs, the planning process will be the same.

Select your chart and type of fabric. Determine the finished dimensions of the stitched area. Divide the number of stitches in width by the number of stitches per inch of fabric. This tells you how many inches wide the design will be. Repeat for height of the design. Or, for an approximate size, refer to the chart (**Fig 6**) on page 6.

Add enough additional fabric for desired unworked area around the design plus an additional 2" or 3" on each side for use in finishing and mounting.

Cut your fabric exactly true, right along the holes of the fabric. Some ravelling will occur as you handle the fabric; however, an overcast basting stitch, machine zigzag stitch, or masking tape around the raw edges will minimize ravelling.

Ideally, the progression of your work should be from left to right and from the top of the design (and fabric) toward the bottom. With this sequence, you will bring your thread up from the back to the front through unoccupied fabric holes and will stitch down from front to back through already occupied holes, thereby disturbing completed stitches as little as possible.

Finishing

When you have finished stitching, dampen your embroidery (or, if soiled, wash in lukewarm mild soapsuds and rinse well). Roll in a towel to remove excess moisture. Place face down on a dry towel or padded surface and press carefully until dry and smooth. Make sure all thread ends are well anchored and clipped closely. Proceed with desired finishing.

Design Index

This index will help you locate designs by subject matter.
Numbers refer to the design's number (not the page number).

Alphabets
90, 182, 270, 365

Angels
141, 290, 321, 351, 355, 357, 362

Animals
6, 32, 33, 52, 64, 65, 66, 67, 68, 83, 87, 200, 222, 228, 230, 236, 252, 267, 270, 275, 285, 304, 312, 314, 324, 346, 349

Babies
77, 270, 350

Baskets
4, 157, 168, 198, 238, 253

Bees, Bugs, Butterflies
21, 40, 42, 43, 44, 80, 93, 95, 112, 120, 148, 161, 164, 171, 267

Birds
5, 14, 24, 28, 31, 40, 59, 79, 82, 116, 119, 123, 140, 162, 209, 211, 213, 229, 278, 306, 317, 318, 345, 363

Borders & Corners
12, 15, 21, 22, 61, 64, 80, 106, 123, 139, 183, 192, 199, 201, 255, 257

Bows
6, 20, 23, 28, 30, 31, 65, 66, 80, 85, 221, 252, 265, 266, 268, 269, 270, 337, 340, 349, 362

Boys & Men
2, 23, 54, 91, 130, 147, 149, 174, 217, 220, 245, 275, 319, 332

Bunnies
6, 83, 200, 267

Buildings
36, 60, 142, 187, 240, 259, 262, 263, 264, 283, 309, 323

Celestial
8, 117, 122, 270

Chickens, Ducks, Geese
7, 18, 30, 46, 58, 151, 158, 166, 268, 269, 270, 289, 294, 303, 331

Christmas
288, 290, 293, 300, 301, 325, 326, 327, 328, 329, 330, 331, 334, 335, 336, 337, 338, 340, 342, 343, 344, 345, 348, 351, 354, 355, 357, 358, 359, 360, 361, 364, 365

Clowns
62, 270

Country
2, 3, 34, 41, 54, 55, 58, 97, 106, 147, 151, 158, 166, 170, 176, 178, 186, 187, 188, 209,

Country *(continued)*
233, 234, 235, 237, 240, 242, 244, 245, 246, 247, 258, 271, 272, 283, 303, 332, 333

Easter
4, 6, 7, 18, 83, 267

Fairies & Fantasy
26, 113, 204, 274, 279, 299

Family
20, 23, 147

Fish
104, 105

Flowers & Plants
4, 9, 10, 11, 15, 16, 17, 19, 20, 21, 22, 27, 29, 31, 33, 34, 35, 37, 39, 40, 45, 46, 47, 48, 49, 50, 51, 53, 54, 55, 56, 57, 61, 63, 69, 70, 71, 72, 73, 74, 75, 80, 81, 84, 85, 86, 88, 89, 90, 92, 95, 98, 99, 100, 103, 106, 107, 109, 110, 115, 120, 124, 125, 126, 132, 137, 143, 144, 145, 150, 153, 154, 155, 156, 157, 159, 160, 163, 165, 167, 168, 169, 171, 172, 175, 181, 182, 192, 196, 197, 198, 199, 202, 205, 208, 221, 235, 238, 241, 243, 248, 252, 254, 255, 256, 261, 267, 270, 273, 277, 329, 360, 364, 365

Food
13, 94, 102, 127, 128, 129, 131, 134, 135, 136, 138, 139, 170, 177, 178, 180, 183, 184, 185, 188, 189, 195, 203, 206, 214, 218, 219, 223, 227, 231, 234, 235, 239, 249, 250, 253, 257

Fruits
13, 94, 128, 129, 136, 139, 170, 177, 178, 180, 188, 195, 203, 218, 225, 227, 231, 234, 235, 239, 249, 250, 253, 257, 338, 345

Gardens & Gardening
9, 38, 50, 115, 118, 142, 167, 175, 194, 247

Girls & Women
3, 20, 34, 55, 76, 91, 147, 179, 181, 216, 246, 333

Halloween
228, 232

Hearts
12, 17, 39, 51, 53, 56, 60, 68, 72, 76, 78, 86, 87, 107, 125, 172, 173, 175, 176, 186, 188, 202, 245, 246, 248, 255, 258, 270, 290, 302, 313, 322, 331, 332, 333, 347, 350, 352, 359, 361, 362

Holidays
4, 6, 7, 18, 83, 96, 211, 216, 217, 219, 231, 232, 267, 280, 288, 290, 293, 300, 301, 325, 326, 327, 328, 329, 330, 331, 334, 335, 336, 337, 338, 340, 342, 343, 344, 345, 348, 351, 354, 355, 357, 358, 359, 360, 361, 364, 365

Home Sentiments
60, 72, 146, 173, 207, 241, 302, 352, 353

Houses
24, 25, 41, 97, 152, 173, 186, 191, 207, 212, 233, 242, 244, 260, 276, 286, 298, 306, 307, 308, 309, 310, 311, 313, 322, 335

Inspirational
190, 194, 236, 241

July 4th
96

Lambs
33, 64, 67, 68, 87, 236, 270

Landscapes
25, 36, 38, 41, 142, 152, 162, 191, 286, 287, 298, 305

Leaves
193, 200, 201, 203, 210, 224, 225, 226, 293, 318, 360

Quilting
57, 146, 237, 243, 328

Rainbows & Sunsets
101, 111, 114, 121

Sayings & Sentiments
16, 17, 20, 23, 27, 30, 31, 40, 45, 60, 67, 72, 78, 91, 93, 107, 108, 111, 130, 146, 173, 178, 186, 190, 193, 194, 197, 202, 207, 218, 236, 241, 254, 282, 302, 304, 315, 320, 322, 324, 335, 344, 347, 352, 353

Snowmen & Snowflakes
281, 292, 295, 296, 297, 315, 321, 336

Sports
101, 108, 130, 133, 174, 215, 220, 284, 291, 316, 319

Teddy Bears
52, 65, 66, 222, 252, 270, 304

Thanksgiving
211, 216, 217, 219, 231

Toys
1, 52, 65, 66, 222, 251, 252, 270, 304, 339, 341, 344, 346, 354, 356

Vegetables
102, 127, 131, 134, 135, 138, 189, 206, 214, 216, 217, 219, 223, 231

Welcomes & Guest
78, 170, 261, 271

Wreaths
10, 39, 56, 165, 172, 182, 300, 301, 327, 338

Spring

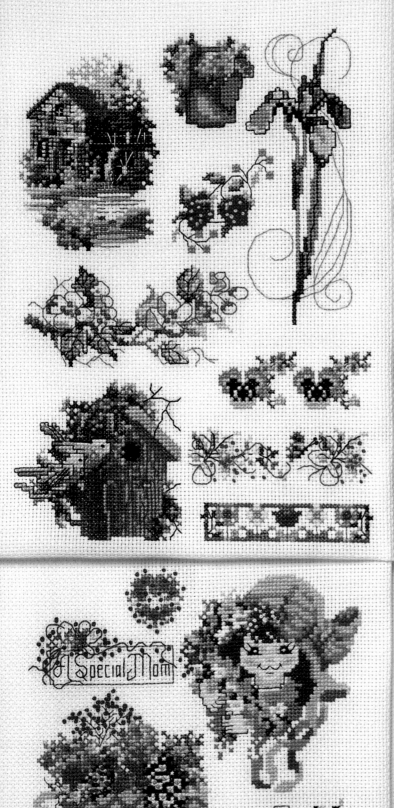

A Special Mom

SPRING

Spring

Spring

Spring

Happy
SPRING

April showers
bring May
flowers

a very
SPECIAL
FATHER

RAIN RAIN GO AWAY

It's
Spring

I ♥ Spring

Spring Design Directory

The charts are in numerical order beginning on page 14.

page 9

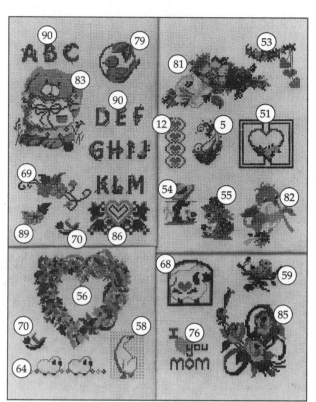

page 10

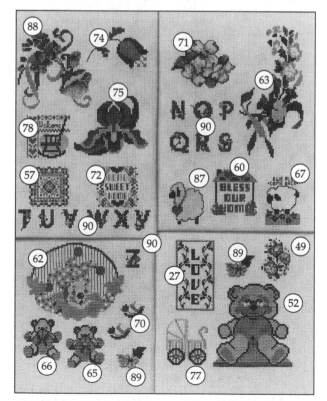

page 11

page 12

1 Flyin' High
(19 wide x 34 high)

		Anchor	DMC
▫	= white	1	blanc
✧	= pink	52	957
●	= red	19	304
☆	= lt orange	311	3827
#	= med orange	323	3825
★	= dk orange	330	947
◉	= yellow	291	444
◆	= green	238	703
■	= blue	146	798
▲	= gray	401	413
│	= Backstitch:		

face outline, rays—red
eyebrows, eyes, nose, mouth,
kite—gray

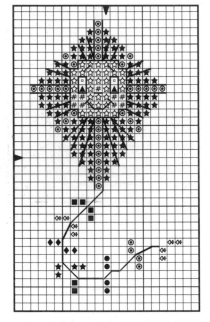

2 Overall Sam
(23 wide x 28 high)

		Anchor	DMC
✧	= pink	26	894
~	= lt peach	1012	754
	dk peach	8	3824
○	= lt orange	323	3825
◉	= dk orange	330	947
▫	= yellow	289	307
☆	= lt gold	361	738
★	= med gold	363	436
◇	= yellow-green	256	704
◆	= green	269	936
□	= lt blue	129	809
■	= dk blue	132	797
▲	= rust	370	434
│	= Backstitch:		

face, hands—dk peach
stems—yellow-green
pants—dk blue

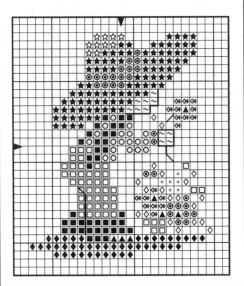

3 Sunbonnet Sue
(25 wide x 29 high)

		Anchor	DMC
▫	= white	1	blanc
✧	= pink	26	894
~	= peach	1012	754
☆	= lt orange	323	3825
#	= med orange	324	721
★	= dk orange	330	947
+	= yellow	289	307
◇	= yellow-green	256	704
◆	= green	269	936
ω	= blue	129	809
♡	= lt purple	103	211
♥	= med purple	92	553
▲	= rust	370	434
│	= Backstitch: med orange		

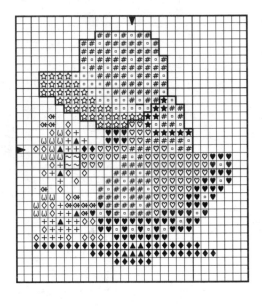

4 Easter Basket
(31 wide x 32 high)

		Anchor	DMC
♡	= lt pink	24	963
♥	= med pink	26	894
☆	= lt orange	323	3825
★	= dk orange	330	947
∧	= lt gold	891	676
⊞	= dk gold	308	781
◇	= lt green	255	907
◆	= med green	239	702
○	= lt turquoise	928	3811
●	= dk turquoise	168	3810
△	= lt purple	342	211
▲	= med purple	109	209
~	= lt taupe	376	3774
×	= med taupe	378	841
■	= dk taupe	936	632
│	= Backstitch:		

bow knot—dk gold
basket—med taupe
ribbon—dk taupe

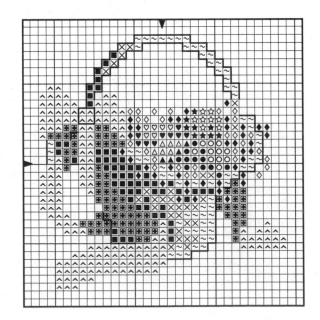

5 Snug In Her Nest
(19 wide x 29 high)

		Anchor	DMC
▫ =	white	1	blanc
☆ =	lt red	35	3801
▲ =	med red	47	321
▽ =	yellow	305	743
✵ =	gold	307	783
○ =	lt green	238	703
◆ =	dk green	245	986
◇ =	lt blue	976	3752
	dk blue	978	312
■ =	brown	370	434
• =	French Knots: dk blue		
┃ =	Backstitch:		
	stems—dk green		
	leaves, bird—brown		

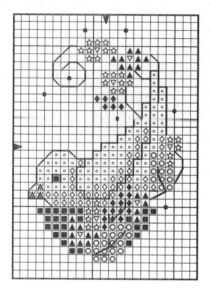

6 Bunny & Bow
(19 wide x 31 high)

		Anchor	DMC
▫ =	white	1	blanc
♡ =	lt pink	50	605
♥ =	dk pink	52	957
◆ =	green	225	702
~ =	very lt brown	276	739
△ =	lt brown	376	3774
+ =	med brown	379	840
◐ =	med dk brown	359	801
▲ =	very dk brown	381	938
■ =	black	403	310
• =	French Knot: white		
┃ =	Backstitch:		
	bow—dk pink		
	ear, chin, mouth—med brown		
	eye—black		

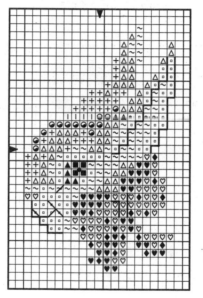

7 Ready For Easter
(20 wide x 20 high)

		Anchor	DMC
~ =	lt peach	9575	3830
◉ =	dk peach	337	3776
☆ =	lt gold	361	738
★ =	med gold	363	436
	dk gold	365	435
	green	923	3818
♡ =	lt purple	95	554
# =	med purple	98	553
♥ =	dk purple	101	550
	black	403	310
• =	French Knot: black		
┃ =	Backstitch:		
	chick—dk gold		
	grass—green		

8 Sunny Face
(35 wide x 35 high)

		Anchor	DMC
☆ =	lt orange	295	726
# =	med orange	330	947
★ =	dk orange	333	608
~ =	very lt yellow	890	729
◐ =	med yellow	291	444
✤ =	med brown	309	781
■ =	dk brown	359	801
• =	French Knots: med orange		
\ =	Straight Stitch: med orange (rays)		
┃ =	Backstitch:		
	eyebrows, mouth—med brown		
	nose—med brown (2 strands)		
	eyes, eyelashes—dk brown		

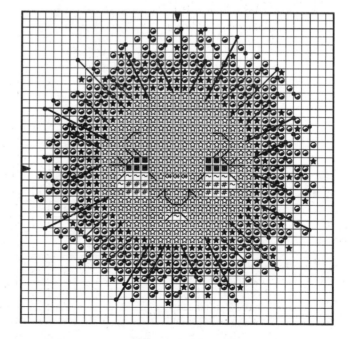

9 Flower Cart
(48 wide x 58 high)

		Anchor	DMC
▫	= white	1	blanc
O	= lt pink	24	963
⧎	= dk pink	27	899
⊖	= lt red	35	3801
●	= med red	19	304
△	= med orange	323	3825
▲	= dk orange	326	720
☆	= med yellow	295	726
★	= dk yellow	298	972
~	= yellow-green	255	907
◇	= lt green	1043	369
#	= med green	258	905
◆	= dk green	1044	895
∞	= lt turquoise	928	3811
◈	= med turquoise	168	3810
⊘	= lt blue	175	809
⬗	= dk blue	940	792
✳	= blue-green	877	3815
U	= lt purple	95	554
⊞	= med purple	98	553
♡	= lt fuchsia	85	3609
♥	= dk fuchsia	88	718
⋈	= rust	355	975
□	= lt brown	366	951
©	= med brown	369	435
■	= dk brown	358	801

• = French Knots:
   in white & turquoise flowers—dk
      yellow
   above flowers—dk fuchsia
   in yellow & orange flowers—rust

| = Backstitch: blue-green

10 Mini Wreath
(15 wide x 16 high)

		Anchor	DMC
⧎	= pink	27	899
★	= orange	329	3340
☆	= yellow	295	726
◆	= green	226	703
ω	= blue	161	813
✕	= purple	96	3609
	brown	370	434

• = French Knots: brown

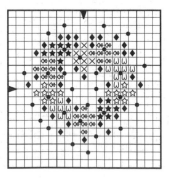

11 Hyacinth
(15 wide x 24 high)

		Anchor	DMC
▫	= lt pink	75	962
⧎	= med pink	27	899
◇	= lt green	213	504
#	= med green	215	320
◆	= dk green	218	319
♡	= lt purple	342	211
♥	= med purple	110	208
✕	= brown	371	434

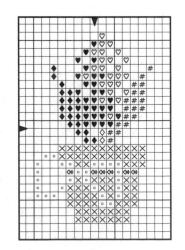

12 Heartpath
(13 wide x 33 high)

		Anchor	DMC
O	= pink	40	956
◆	= green	238	703
☆	= blue	131	798
⧎	= gray	399	318

13 Strawberries

(27 wide x 27 high)

		Anchor	DMC
✿	= pink	26	894
♥	= red	9046	321
	yellow	305	743
◇	= lt green	240	966
♦	= med green	244	702
	dk green	246	986
•	= French Knots: yellow		
|	= Backstitch: dk green		

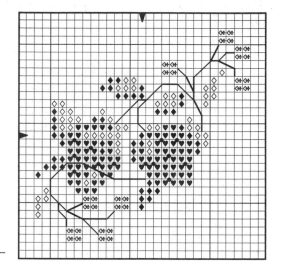

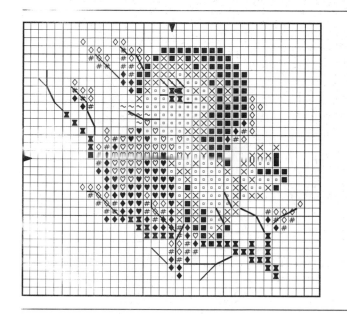

14 Baby Red Breast

(33 wide x 30 high)

		Anchor	DMC
	white	1	blanc
♡	= lt pink	8	3824
♥	= dk pink	10	351
~	= peach	363	436
0	= lt green	240	966
#	= med green	243	703
♦	= dk green	246	986
▫	= lt brown	366	951
✕	= med brown	369	435
■	= dk brown	359	801
✕	= very dk brown	381	938

• = French Knot: white
| = Backstitch:
    leaf veins—dk
     green
    beak, bird—dk
     brown
    branches, stems,
     eye—very dk
     brown

15 Spring Flower Corner

(39 wide x 51 high)

		Anchor	DMC
~	= very lt rose	892	225
O	= lt rose	968	778
✿	= med rose	970	3726
●	= dk rose	972	3803
★	= yellow	289	307
▢	= lt yellow-green	260	772
#	= med yellow-green	261	989
■	= dk yellow-green	263	3362
◇	= lt green	242	989
♦	= dk green	245	986
△	= lt blue-green	875	3813
▲	= med blue-green	877	3815
♡	= lt blue	120	3747
✕	= med blue	176	793
♥	= dk blue	178	791
	brown	360	898

| = Backstitch:
    rose flower—med rose
    stems—dk yellow-green
    border—brown

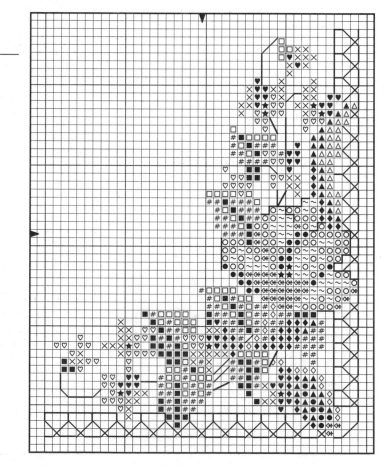

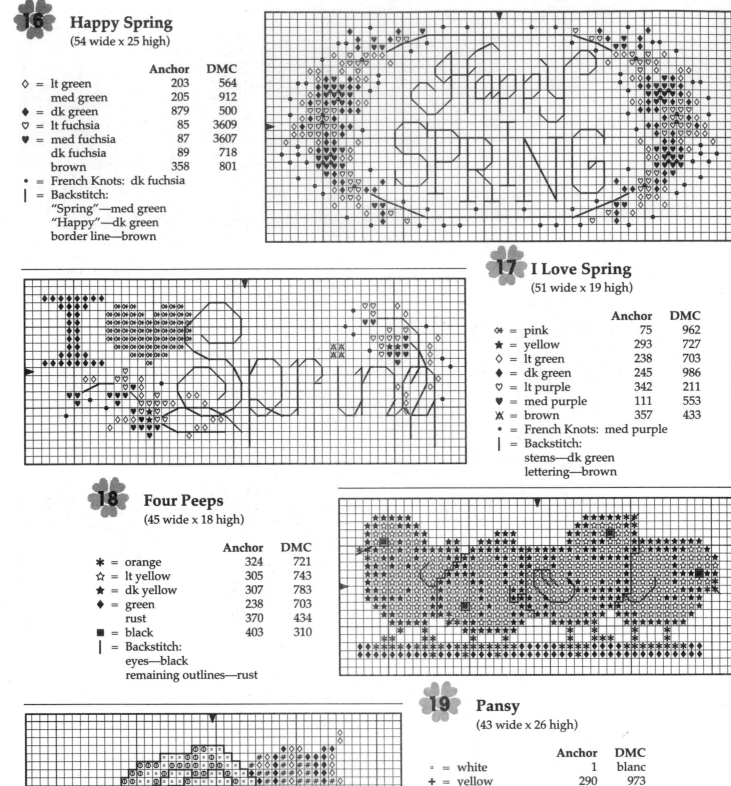

16 Happy Spring
(54 wide x 25 high)

		Anchor	DMC
◇ =	lt green	203	564
	med green	205	912
◆ =	dk green	879	500
♡ =	lt fuchsia	85	3609
♥ =	med fuchsia	87	3607
	dk fuchsia	89	718
	brown	358	801

• = French Knots: dk fuchsia
| = Backstitch:
 "Spring"—med green
 "Happy"—dk green
 border line—brown

17 I Love Spring
(51 wide x 19 high)

		Anchor	DMC
✿ =	pink	75	962
★ =	yellow	293	727
◇ =	lt green	238	703
◆ =	dk green	245	986
♡ =	lt purple	342	211
♥ =	med purple	111	553
✕ =	brown	357	433

• = French Knots: med purple
| = Backstitch:
 stems—dk green
 lettering—brown

18 Four Peeps
(45 wide x 18 high)

		Anchor	DMC
✳ =	orange	324	721
☆ =	lt yellow	305	743
★ =	dk yellow	307	783
◆ =	green	238	703
	rust	370	434
■ =	black	403	310

| = Backstitch:
 eyes—black
 remaining outlines—rust

19 Pansy
(43 wide x 26 high)

		Anchor	DMC
□ =	white	1	blanc
+ =	yellow	290	973
◇ =	lt green	240	966
# =	med green	243	703
◆ =	dk green	1044	895
✳ =	purple	112	552
◍ =	lt tan	366	951
	med tan	370	434
■ =	blue-black	152	939

| = Backstitch:
 inside the petals—purple
 separation between purple areas—
   lt tan
 petal outlines—med tan

20 **A Special Mom**
(40 wide x 18 high)

			Anchor	DMC
✤	=	lt rose	75	962
		dk rose	78	3685
★	=	yellow	295	726
◆	=	green	227	701
♥	=	purple	110	208
		brown	359	801
•	=	French Knots:		
		pink flower—yellow		
		in yellow flower—brown		
		remaining knots—dk rose		
		=	Backstitch:		
		ribbon—dk rose		

border line—green
lettering—brown

21 **Ladybug Border**
(53 wide x 12 high)

			Anchor	DMC
▫	=	white	1	blanc
✤	=	pink	52	957
♥	=	red	9046	321
◆	=	green	244	702
■	=	black	403	310
•	=	French Knots:		
		scattered—pink		
		eyes—black		
		=	Backstitch:		
		stems—green		
		between wings—black		

22 **Pansy Duet**
(20-wide repeat x 15 high)

			Anchor	DMC
▫	=	white	1	blanc
☆	=	med yellow	290	973
★	=	dk yellow	307	783
◇	=	lt green	875	3813
◆	=	dk green	877	3815
○	=	lt rust	881	945
✕	=	med rust	9575	3830
●	=	dk rust	1049	3826
■	=	black	403	310
		=	Backstitch: dk green		

23 **A Very Special Father**
(52 wide x 33 high)

			Anchor	DMC
◆	=	green	217	561
		med turquoise	187	958
		dk turquoise	189	943
		blue	940	792
•	=	French Knots: blue		
		=	Backstitch:		
		"a very," "Father"—green		
		tracery border—med turquoise		
		"special"—dk turquoise		

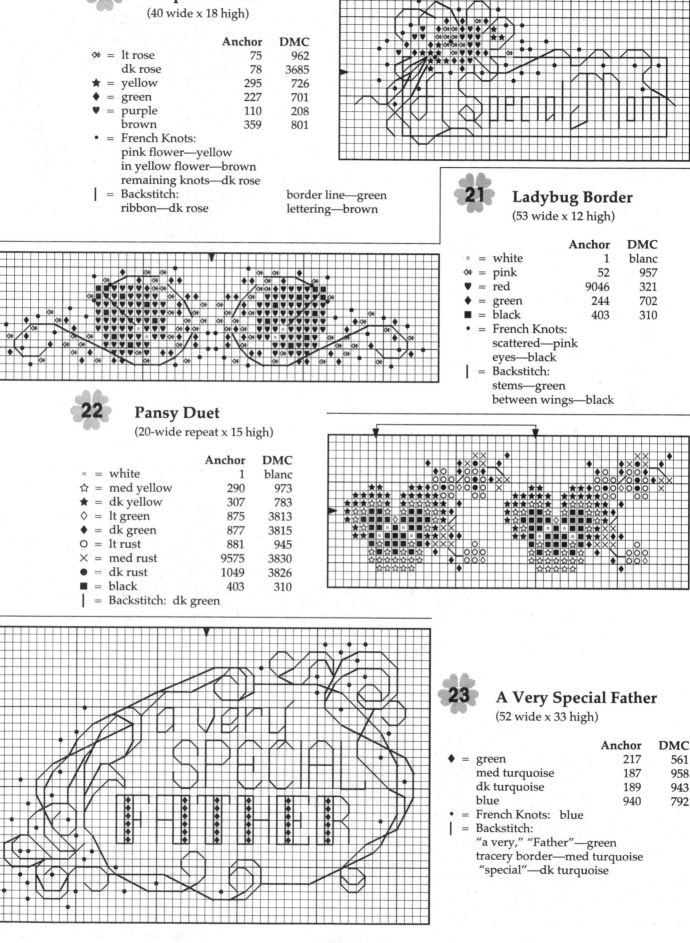

24 Bluebird House
(45 wide x 43 high)

		Anchor	DMC
♡	= lt pink	36	3326
✿	= med pink	68	3687
♥	= dk pink	70	902
⊥	= rose	895	223
△	= peach	337	3776
◇	= lt green	240	966
#	= med green	243	703
◆	= dk green	246	986
O	= very lt blue	1037	3756
✕	= lt blue	9159	828
◉	= med blue	1039	518
▫	= very lt rust	880	951
~	= lt rust	882	758
⊞	= med rust	884	356
◣	= dk rust	371	434
⧖	= very dk rust	352	300
□	= lt brown	376	3774
⋈	= med brown	379	840
■	= dk brown	382	3371
✐	= lt taupe	390	3033
✎	= med taupe	392	642
	dk taupe	905	3021
	black	403	310

• = French Knots: black
| = Backstitch:
  front of birdhouse—
    dk rust
  branches—dk brown
  beak, tail feathers,
    wings—dk taupe

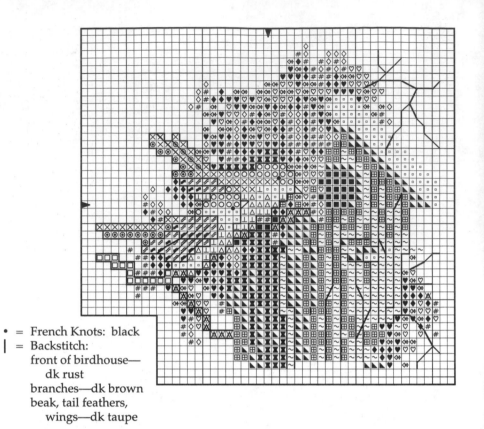

25 Spring Homestead
(58 wide x 61 high)

		Anchor	DMC
♡	= lt pink	26	894
♥	= dk pink	28	892
★	= orange	329	3340
☆	= yellow	290	973
✐	= lt yellow-green	253	472
⊞	= med yellow-green	255	907
✎	= med dk yellow-green	258	905
◇	= lt green	259	772
#	= med green	262	3363
◆	= dk green	1044	895
✿	= med blue-green	876	3816
⋊	= dk blue-green	878	501
✕	= turquoise	168	3810
∞	= lt blue	128	800
⧖	= med blue	131	798
⬠	= lt purple	110	208
♠	= med purple	112	552
□	= lt blue-gray	848	927
⊥	= med blue-gray	850	926
■	= dk blue-gray	851	3808
−	= very lt brown	372	738
△	= lt brown	374	420
⊕	= med brown	944	434
▲	= dk brown	360	898
∧	= lt taupe	899	3782
◉	= med taupe	393	640
⧗	= very dk taupe	1041	844

• = French Knots:
  in dk blue-green bushes—dk pink
  in med blue-green bushes—yellow
| = Backstitch:
  windows—very lt brown

26 Spring Fairy
(52 wide x 99 high)

			Anchor	DMC
▫	=	white/filament	6/032	blanc/032
━	=	very lt pink	271	819
♡	=	lt pink	24	963
❄	=	med pink	75	962
		dk pink	76	961
♥	=	rose	68	3687
~	=	lt peach	1011	948
⧖	=	dk peach	1012	754
◉	=	orange	337	3776
★	=	yellow/filament	295/032	726/032
		yellow-green	258	905
◇	=	lt green	1043	369
#	=	med green	244	702
◆	=	dk green	1044	895
✕	=	blue/filament	130/032	809/032
ⱳ	=	purple/filament	108/032	210/032
∧	=	tan/filament	942/032	738/032
		brown	936	632

Note: For wings, use two strands of floss and one strand of pearl (032) blending filament.

| = Backstitch:
flower blossom hat—dk pink
face, hands, legs—orange
flowing robe—yellow-green
eyes, mouth—brown (2 strands)

27 Love
(25 wide x 47 high)

			Anchor	DMC
❄	=	lt pink	26	894
♥	=	dk pink	59	326
✛	=	green	217	561
☐	=	lt brown	368	437
■	=	med brown	370	434
		= Backstitch: green		

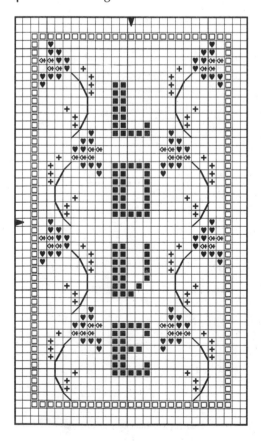

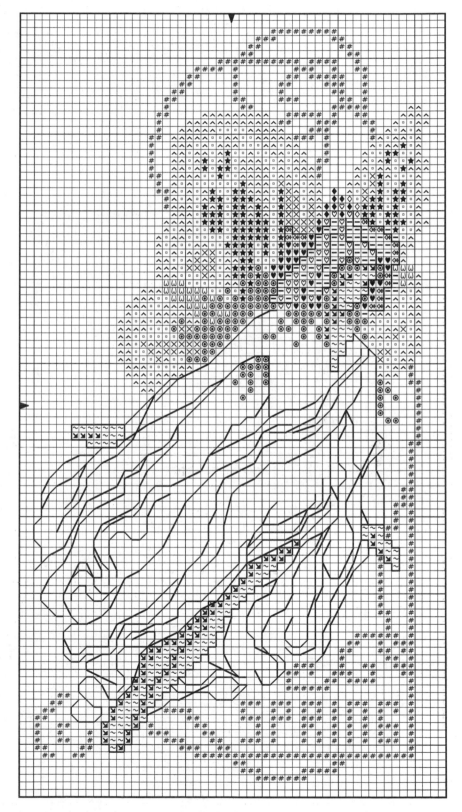

21

28 Chubby Cheeks

(60 wide x 33 high)

		Anchor	DMC
▫	= white	1	blanc
○	= very lt pink	48	3689
✿	= med pink	50	605
●	= very dk pink	62	3806
▲	= pink-orange	1024	3328
☆	= lt yellow	295	726
◉	= med yellow	291	444
★	= dk yellow	307	783
✕	= yellow-green	269	936
◇	= lt green	1043	369
#	= med green	243	703
◆	= dk green	1044	895
–	= very lt blue	128	800
□	= lt blue	130	809
✕	= med blue	131	798
■	= blue-black	152	939
^	= gray	398	415
	= Backstitch:		

eyes, eyelashes, mouths—blue-black
bows, between heads—gray

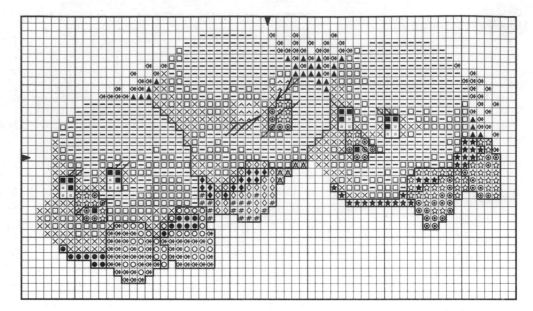

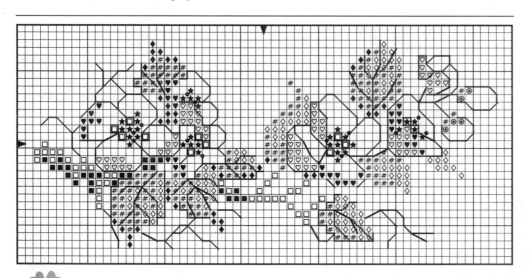

29 Dogwood

(60 wide x 27 high)

		Anchor	DMC
♡	= lt pink	1021	761
♥	= dk pink	1024	3328
★	= yellow	295	726
◇	= lt green	259	772
#	= med green	261	989
◆	= dk green	263	3362
◉	= purple	1018	3726
□	= med brown	378	841
■	= dk brown	936	632
•	= French Knots: med brown		
	= Backstitch:		

blossoms, stamens, flower
centers—dk pink
leaves—dk green
branches—med brown

30 Rain Rain Go Away

(54 wide x 36 high)

		Anchor	DMC
▫	= white	1	blanc
△	= lt orange	324	721
▲	= dk orange	326	720
★	= yellow	290	973
	gold	309	781
+	= yellow-green	253	472
◇	= lt green	203	564
◆	= dk green	205	912
○	= lt blue	128	800
✿	= med blue	130	809
●	= dk blue	132	797
~	= tan	367	738
■	= brown	381	938
	= Backstitch:		

blue bow—white
yellow bow—gold
green bow—dk green
raindrops—lt blue
lettering—dk blue
eyes, beak—brown

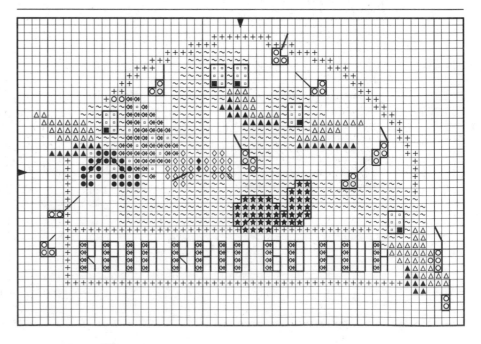

31 It's Spring

(61 wide x 36 high)

		Anchor	DMC
⊕ =	pink	50	605
O =	lt orange	313	742
✕ =	med orange	314	741
● =	dk orange	316	970
☆ =	lt yellow	295	726
	med yellow	291	444
★ =	med gold	306	783
	dk gold	308	781
◇ =	lt green	238	703
# =	med green	244	702
◆ =	dk green	1044	895
◉ =	blue	140	3755
✳ =	fuchsia	86	3608
■ =	brown	358	801
	=	Backstitch:		

ribbon—med yellow
  (2 strands)
feathers—dk gold
apostrophe—lt green
eyes, beak—brown

32 Spring Fawn

(68 wide x 61 high)

		Anchor	DMC
~ =	white	1	blanc
★ =	yellow	288	445

		Anchor	DMC
∧ =	very lt yellow-green	259	772
△ =	lt yellow-green	253	472
⊕ =	med yellow-green	255	907
⊞ =	med dk yellow-green	258	905
⊠ =	dk yellow-green	269	936
◇ =	lt green	242	989
◆ =	med green	244	702
O =	lt blue	121	809
# =	med blue	122	3807
● =	dk blue	123	820
☐ =	lt brown	933	543
✕ =	med brown	378	841
■ =	dk brown	936	632
	=	Backstitch:		

(fern) fiddlehead —med dk
  yellow-green
stems, leaves—dk yellow-green
fawn—dk brown

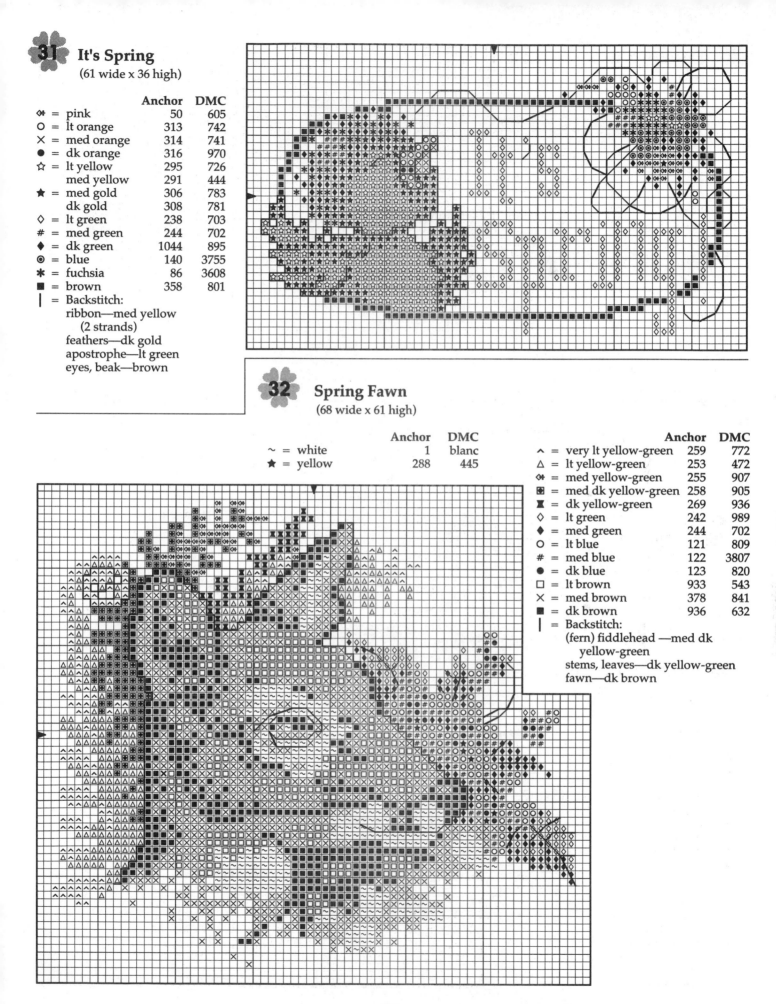

23

33 Frolicking Lamb

(48 wide x 38 high)

		Anchor	DMC
▫	= white	1	blanc
O	= lt pink	24	963
⊕	= med pink	26	894
☆	= lt orange	313	742
★	= med orange	314	741
∞	= lt yellow	301	744
=	= med yellow	890	729
▽	= very lt yellow-green	253	472
⌇	= lt yellow-green	255	907
⌐	= med yellow-green	267	469
⊠	= dk yellow-green	269	936
◇	= lt green	1043	369
#	= med green	242	989
◆	= dk green	246	986
✥	= med blue	167	519
✳	= dk blue	1039	518
♡	= lt purple	342	211
♥	= med purple	110	208
~	= lt brown	376	3774
✕	= med brown	379	840
	dk brown	936	632
−	= lt gray	397	3024
⊠	= med gray	235	414
⋈	= dk gray	401	413
■	= black	403	310

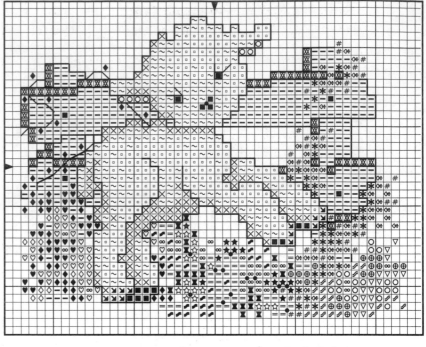

• = French Knots:
 nose highlight—white
 flower centers—dk brown

| = Backstitch:
 vine—dk green
 lamb outline—dk brown
 fence—dk gray
 eyes, eyelashes—black

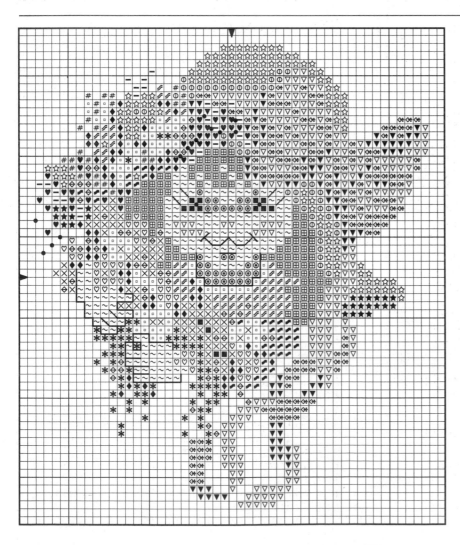

34 Flower Girl

(49 wide x 58 high)

		Anchor	DMC
▫	= white	1	blanc
▽	= lt pink	24	963
✥	= med pink	26	894
▼	= dk pink	28	892
~	= lt peach	1009	3770
⊙	= dk peach	1012	754
✳	= orange	328	3341
✕	= yellow	290	973
☆	= lt gold	361	738
⊕	= med gold	363	436
★	= dk gold	365	435
−	= lt yellow-green	253	472
#	= med yellow-green	255	907
◇	= med green	242	989
◆	= dk green	246	986
⌇	= lt blue	1038	519
⌐	= dk blue	1039	518
♡	= lt purple	95	554
♥	= dk purple	100	327
⊞	= med brown	359	801
■	= dk brown	380	838

• = French Knots:
 eyes, dk purple flowers above
  head—white
 remaining—dk purple

| = Backstitch:
 mouth, chin, hands—med brown
 eyes, eyelashes—dk brown

35 Wishing Well

(32 wide x 48 high)

		Anchor	DMC
▫ =	white	1	blanc
✲ =	pink	50	605
♡ =	lt rose	66	3688
⊙ =	med rose	68	3687
♥ =	dk rose	69	3350
☆ =	yellow	305	743
◇ =	med green	209	913
◆ =	dk green	211	562
∞ =	lt purple	342	211
✐ =	med purple	109	209
✐ =	dk purple	112	552
— =	tan	366	951
△ =	lt brown	358	801
▲ =	dk brown	371	434
^ =	lt gray	234	762
⊠ =	med gray	399	318
⊠ =	dk gray	401	413
	=	Backstitch:		

    roof—dk rose
    stems—dk green
    edges of white areas—med gray
    bricks in well, pail, handle—dk gray

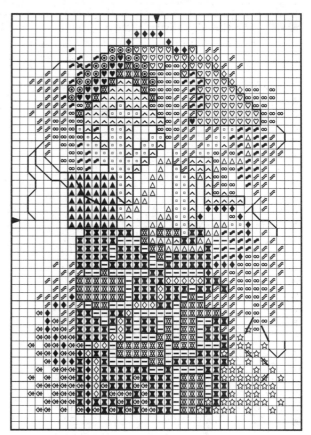

| = Backstitch:
    railing, upper window panes, doorway—white
    water—white/filament (1 strand each)
    roof flowers—med purple
    house, brickwork, lower window—very dk gray

| = water—dk blue-green

36 Old Mill Stream

(38 wide x 52 high)
Note: For cross stitch, use two strands of floss with one strand of filament.

		Anchor	DMC
▫ =	white	1	blanc
= =	white/filament	1/032	blanc/032
O =	lt pink	23	3713
© =	med pink	26	894
☆ =	lt yellow	301	744
★ =	dk yellow	306	783
> =	lt yellow-green	253	472
⊞ =	med yellow-green	255	907
◇ =	lt green	875	3813
# =	med green	877	3815
◆ =	dk green	879	500
▽ =	lt blue-green	1042	504
ω =	med blue-green	185	964
⊠ =	dk blue-green	188	3812
∞ =	lt purple	342	211
✲ =	med purple	110	208
— =	tan	367	738
✐ =	med rust	369	435
✐ =	dk rust	371	434
⊞ =	med brown	358	801
■ =	dk brown	381	938
⊥ =	lt taupe	899	3782
∿ =	med taupe	903	640
^ =	very lt gray	234	762
+ =	med lt gray	398	415
⊙ =	med gray	235	414
⊠ =	dk gray	401	413
⊠ =	very dk gray	236	3799
\ =	Straight Stitch:		

    waterwheel spokes, vertical bridge rails—white

37 Johnny Jump-Ups
(27 wide x 34 high)

	Anchor	DMC
⊙ = med peach	9	352
● = dk peach	10	351
☆ = yellow	295	726
◇ = lt green	203	564
◆ = dk green	205	912
▫ = very lt purple	342	211
♡ = lt purple	109	209
# = med purple	111	553
♥ = dk purple	102	550
	= Backstitch:		
stems—dk green		

38 Mossy Arbor
(35 wide x 48 high)

	Anchor	DMC
✤ = pink	26	894
✱ = orange	329	3340
☆ = yellow	288	445
~ = lt yellow-green	265	3347
# = med yellow-green	267	3346
◪ = dk yellow-green	269	936
◇ = lt green	241	966
◆ = med green	244	702

	Anchor	DMC
♡ = lt purple	103	211
♥ = med purple	97	554
✕ = rust	371	434
■ = med brown	380	838
dk brown	382	3371
	= Backstitch:		
hanging moss—lt yellow-green		
rust tree branches—rust		
vine on brown tree—dk brown		

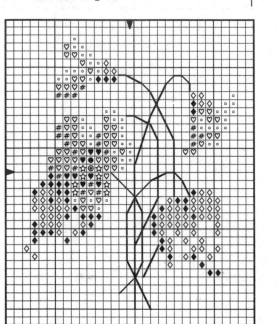

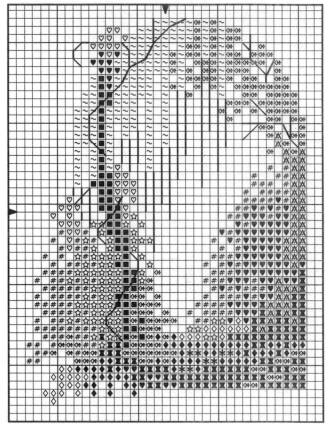

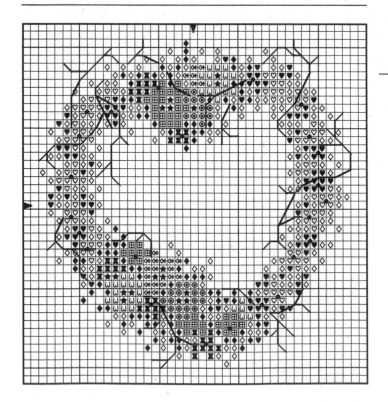

39 Spring Heart Wreath
(39 wide x 41 high)

	Anchor	DMC
✤ = pink	31	3708
◪ = red	1025	347
♡ = lt orange	314	741
♥ = med orange	324	721
★ = yellow	288	445
◇ = lt green	203	564
◆ = dk green	211	562
⊙ = blue	121	809
⊞ = purple	109	209
ω = fuchsia	86	3608
brown	357	433
• = French Knots: yellow		
	= Backstitch: brown		

40

Spring
(72 wide x 25 high)

		Anchor	DMC
▫	= white	1	blanc
✿	= pink	26	894
O	= lt red	1024	3328
◉	= med red	1025	347
✳	= orange	323	3825
☆	= yellow	293	727
◇	= green	257	905
✐	= lt blue	128	800
◤	= med blue	167	519
	dk blue	131	798

		Anchor	DMC
♡	= lt purple	342	211
♥	= dk purple	110	208
✕	= lt brown	368	437
■	= med brown	358	433
	dk brown	359	801
+	= gray	233	452
•	= French Knots:		
	on & near strawberry, in purple		
	flowers (near "S")—yellow		
	scattered with flowers—dk purple		

butterfly—dk brown
bird eyes, antennae—gray

| = Backstitch:
bird beaks—orange
vine & stems near strawberry—green
birds—dk blue
brown branch stems—med brown
lettering—dk brown
antennae, gray branch, stems, nest,
    white blossoms—gray

41

Springtime
On The Farm
(68 wide x 40 high)

		Anchor	DMC
▫	= white	1	blanc
o	= lt pink	48	3689
✿	= med pink	50	605
●	= dk pink	52	957
♡	= lt rose	66	3688
♥	= dk rose	69	3687
∧	= lt mauve	894	223
◉	= dk mauve	897	221
△	= lt red	1022	760
▲	= med red	1025	347
◤	= dk red	44	815
☆	= med yellow	305	743

		Anchor	DMC
★	= dk yellow	307	783
~	= lt gold	311	3827
✳	= med gold	890	729
+	= lt yellow-green	253	472
✕	= med yellow-green	256	704
⊞	= dk yellow-green	258	905
◇	= lt green	1043	369
#	= med green	261	989
◆	= dk green	1044	895
□	= lt blue-green	875	3813
⊞	= med blue-green	876	3816
■	= dk blue-green	878	501

		Anchor	DMC
◿	= lt blue	975	3753
◣	= med blue	977	3755
✐	= lt purple	342	211
◤	= med purple	109	209
∿	= tan	367	738
⊠	= brown	358	801
∞	= lt gray	398	415
✕	= med gray	400	317
•	= French Knots:		
	green hedgerows—dk red		
	green bush—med yellow		

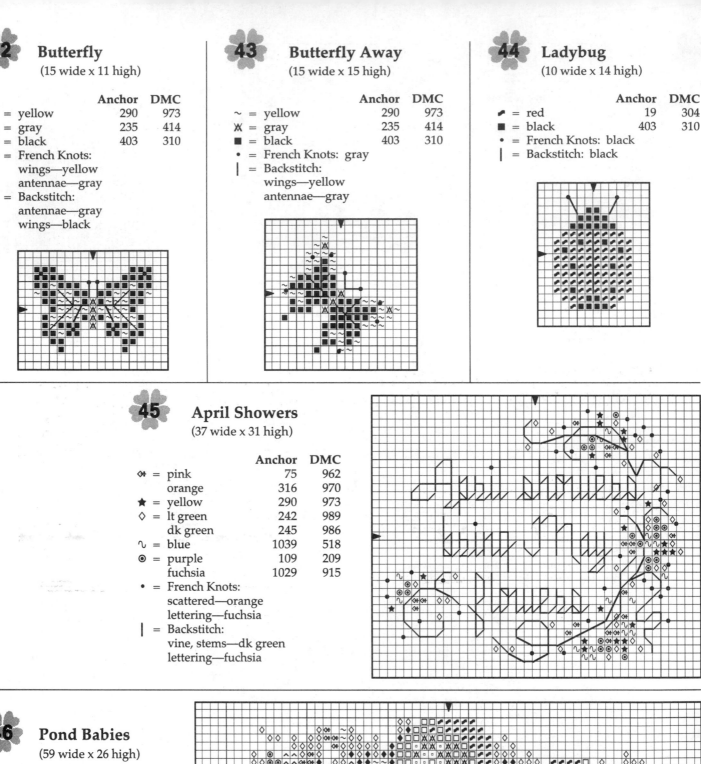

42 **Butterfly**
(15 wide x 11 high)

		Anchor	DMC
~ =	yellow	290	973
⋇ =	gray	235	414
■ =	black	403	310

• = French Knots:
　wings—yellow
　antennae—gray
| = Backstitch:
　antennae—gray
　wings—black

43 **Butterfly Away**
(15 wide x 15 high)

		Anchor	DMC
~ =	yellow	290	973
⋇ =	gray	235	414
■ =	black	403	310

• = French Knots: gray
| = Backstitch:
　wings—yellow
　antennae—gray

44 **Ladybug**
(10 wide x 14 high)

		Anchor	DMC
↙ =	red	19	304
■ =	black	403	310

• = French Knots: black
| = Backstitch: black

45 **April Showers**
(37 wide x 31 high)

		Anchor	DMC
❈ =	pink	75	962
	orange	316	970
★ =	yellow	290	973
◇ =	lt green	242	989
	dk green	245	986
~ =	blue	1039	518
◉ =	purple	109	209
	fuchsia	1029	915

• = French Knots:
　scattered—orange
　lettering—fuchsia
| = Backstitch:
　vine, stems—dk green
　lettering—fuchsia

46 **Pond Babies**
(59 wide x 26 high)

		Anchor	DMC
~ =	lt pink	24	963
❈ =	med pink	31	3708
△ =	lt orange	323	3825
▲ =	med orange	329	3340
▫ =	lt yellow	311	3827
⋇ =	med yellow	363	436
◇ =	lt green	254	3348
◆ =	dk green	257	905
	blue	940	792
∧ =	lt purple	95	554
◉ =	med purple	98	553
□ =	med brown	365	435
↙ =	dk brown	310	780
■ =	brown-black	1041	844

| = Backstitch:　　　　beaks—dk brown
　water—blue　　　　eyes—brown-black

47 Blue Iris
(28 wide x 77 high)

		Anchor	DMC
☆	= med yellow	297	973
	dk yellow	307	783
◇	= lt green	238	703
#	= med green	209	913
◆	= dk green	212	561
~	= very lt blue	1031	3753
O	= lt blue	129	809
⋈	= med blue	131	798
●	= dk blue	134	820
■	= very dk blue	152	939
|	= Backstitch:		
	tracery—dk yellow		
	leaf—dk green		
	iris—very dk blue		

48 Canterbury Bells
(21 wide x 82 high)

		Anchor	DMC
▫	= very lt pink	271	819
❈	= lt pink	25	3326
	med pink	27	899
	med yellow-green	267	469
	dk yellow-green	269	936
◇	= very lt green	1043	369
#	= lt green	241	966
◆	= med green	244	702
∿	= lt purple	108	210
	med purple	110	208
△	= lt rust	1047	402

		Anchor	DMC
▲	= med rust	1049	3826
■	= brown	360	898
•	= French Knots: brown		
|	= Backstitch:		
	pink blossoms—med pink		
	leaves, veins—med		
	yellow-green		
	border lines—dk yellow-green		
	purple blossoms—med purple		
	antennae, wings—brown		

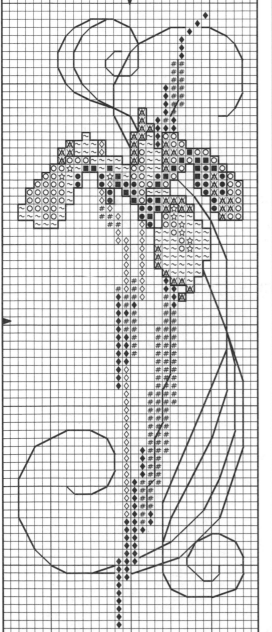

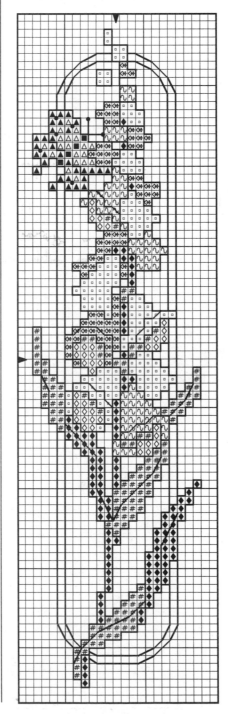

49 Morning Glories
(19 wide x 27 high)

		Anchor	DMC
▫	= white	1	blanc
❈	= pink	26	894
O	= yellow	307	783
★	= green	257	905
△	= lt blue	159	3325
+	= med blue	161	813
▲	= dk blue	162	517
	purple	110	208
•	= French Knots: purple		
|	= Backstitch:		
	stems—green		
	flowers—dk blue		

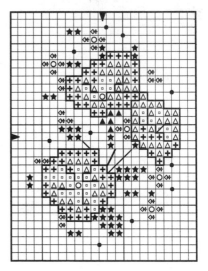

50 Watering Can
(25 wide x 25 high)

			Anchor	DMC
♡	=	lt pink	48	3689
✤	=	med pink	50	605
♥	=	dk pink	52	957
◇	=	lt green	238	703
◆	=	dk green	245	986
□	=	lt blue	928	3811
#	=	med blue	168	3810
■	=	dk blue	169	806
☆	=	med fuchsia	86	3608
★	=	dk fuchsia	87	3607
		gray	401	413
•	=	French Knots: dk blue		
│	=	Backstitch: gray		

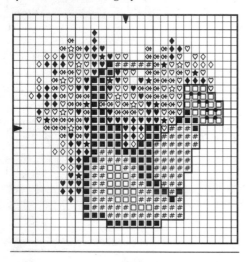

51 Floral Heart
(35 wide x 32 high)

			Anchor	DMC
□	=	lt pink	50	605
♥	=	dk pink	41	956
✳	=	orange	323	3825
▫	=	yellow	305	743
◣	=	green	245	986
◇	=	blue	978	312
✤	=	purple	98	553

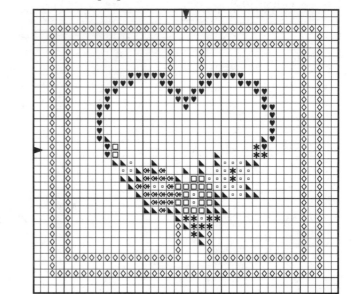

52 Bear
(53 wide x 56 high)

			Anchor	DMC
▫	=	white	1	blanc
✤	=	lt pink	36	3326
◉	=	med pink	27	899
+	=	lt blue	144	800
▼	=	dk blue	146	798
◇	=	tan	366	951
~	=	lt brown	368	437
●	=	dk brown	371	434
☆	=	gray	399	318
■	=	black	403	310

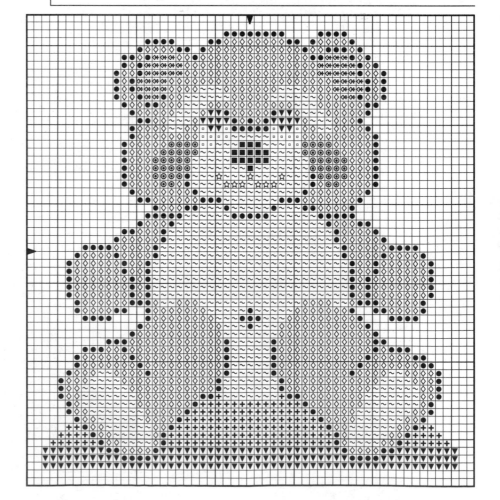

53 Hearts & Garland
(35 wide x 29 high)

		Anchor	DMC
O	= pink	40	956
▫	= yellow	295	726
◆	= green	244	702
✧	= turquoise	187	958
☆	= blue	132	797
✕	= lt purple	96	3609
■	= dk purple	99	553
❘	= Backstitch: dk purple		

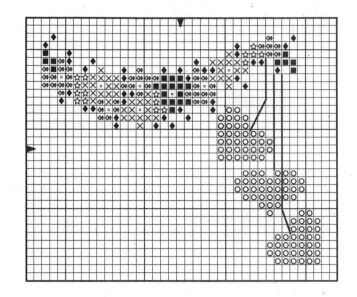

54 Goin' Fishin'
(22 wide x 27 high)

		Anchor	DMC
▫	= peach	6	754
✧	= red	47	321
▽	= orange	323	3825
♡	= lt yellow	295	726
↘	= dk yellow	306	783
□	= lt green	241	966
▼	= dk green	243	703
	blue	976	3752
+	= lt brown	370	434
●	= dk brown	310	780
■	= gray	401	413
❘	= Backstitch:		
	stems—dk green		
	fish, fishing line— blue		
	fishing pole—dk brown		

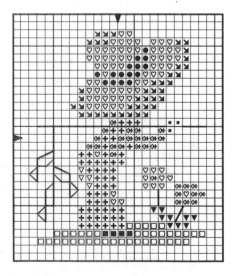

55 How Does Your Garden Grow?
(21 wide x 28 high)

		Anchor	DMC
▫	= peach	6	754
◇	= pink	24	963
✧	= red	47	321
▽	= orange	323	3825
♡	= lt yellow	295	726
↘	= dk yellow	306	783
□	= lt green	241	966
▼	= dk green	243	703
O	= lt blue	976	3752
★	= dk blue	978	312
●	= brown	310	780
❘	= Backstitch:		
	stems—dk green		
	sleeve—lt blue		
	hat—dk blue		

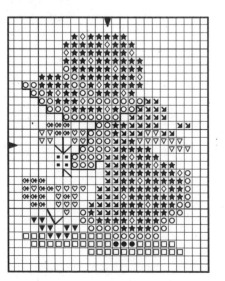

56 **Floral Heart**
(67 wide x 67 high)

		Anchor	DMC				Anchor	DMC
▫	= lt rose	24	963	△	= lt turquoise		185	964
☆	= med rose	27	893	▲	= dk turquoise		188	3812
©	= med orange	313	742	~	= lt blue		136	799
⊕	= dk orange	323	722	✕	= dk blue		139	797
−	= yellow	295	726	O	= lt purple		96	3609
✣	= gold	306	783	★	= dk purple		100	327
◇	= lt green	241	966	+	= brown		370	434
◆	= dk green	228	910					

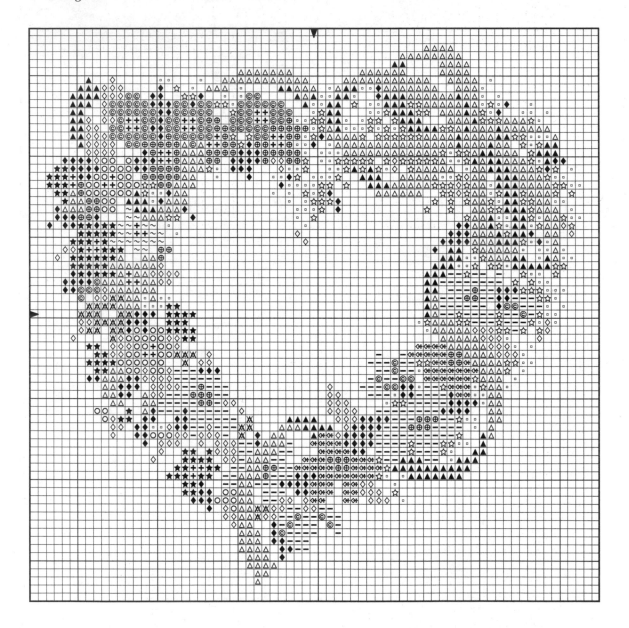

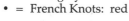

57 Quilter's Flowers
(26 wide x 26 high)

		Anchor	DMC
✥ =	pink	26	894
● =	red	42	326
▫ =	yellow	295	726
☆ =	green	257	905
+ =	blue-gray	976	3752
• =	French Knots: red		

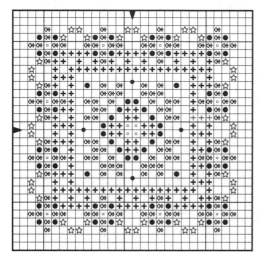

58 Good-Bye, Goose
(23 wide x 31 high)

		Anchor	DMC
▫ =	white	1	blanc
✥ =	pink	24	963
★ =	orange	323	3825
◇ =	blue	976	3752
	gray	235	414
• =	French Knot: gray		
| =	Backstitch: gray		

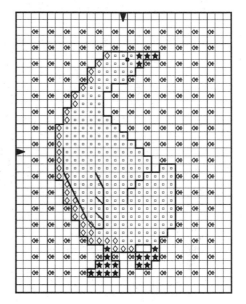

59 Bluebird Of Happiness
(30 wide x 23 high)

		Anchor	DMC
▫ =	lt pink	27	899
✥ =	dk pink	42	326
★ =	orange	324	721
O =	yellow	298	972
□ =	lt green	238	703
⩗ =	dk green	245	986
◇ =	lt blue	159	3325
+ =	med blue	161	813
■ =	dk blue	164	824
⋈ =	brown	370	434
• =	French Knots: brown		
| =	Backstitch:		
	stems—dk green		
	wing—med blue		
	eye—brown		

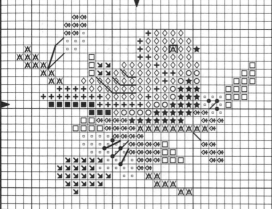

60 Bless Our Home
(31 wide x 30 high)

		Anchor	DMC
● =	med red	35	3801
■ =	dk red	47	321
✕ =	yellow	307	783
⋇ =	med green	265	3347
▲ =	dk green	246	986
▫ =	blue	976	3752

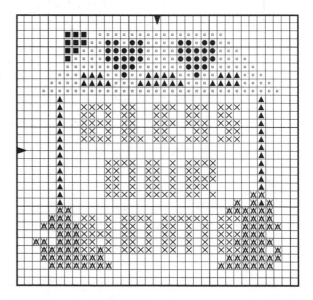

61 Spring Posies
(46 wide x 10 high)

		Anchor	DMC
✔	= lt red	1023	3712
■	= dk red	1025	347
✳	= orange	314	741
~	= lt yellow	295	726
☆	= med yellow	298	972
★	= dk yellow	308	781
◇	= lt green	203	564
#	= med green	205	912
◆	= dk green	923	3818
		= Backstitch:		

flower stems—med green
leaf stems—dk green

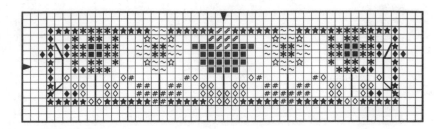

62 Just Clownin' Around
(66 wide x 53 high)

		Anchor	DMC
▫	= white	1	blanc
~	= lt pink	48	818
◇	= med pink	26	894
✔	= dk pink	59	326
☆	= yellow	298	972
▲	= green	243	703
=	= lt blue	130	809
+	= med blue	132	797

		Anchor	DMC
★	= purple	98	553
	gray	236	3799
•	= French Knots: white		
		= Backstitch:		

costume—med pink
background—green
eyes, mouth—gray

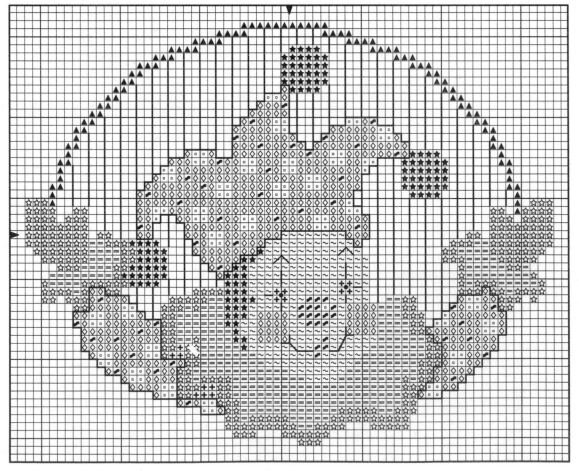

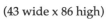

63 **Flower Garden**
(43 wide x 86 high)

		Anchor	DMC
^	= white	1	blanc
~	= lt pink	8	353
❖	= med pink	35	3801
▩	= dk pink	19	321
□	= yellow	305	743
△	= lt yellow-green	264	3348
▲	= dk yellow-green	267	3346
–	= med green	261	989 .
+	= dk green	245	986
*	= blue	160	3325
●	= purple	119	333

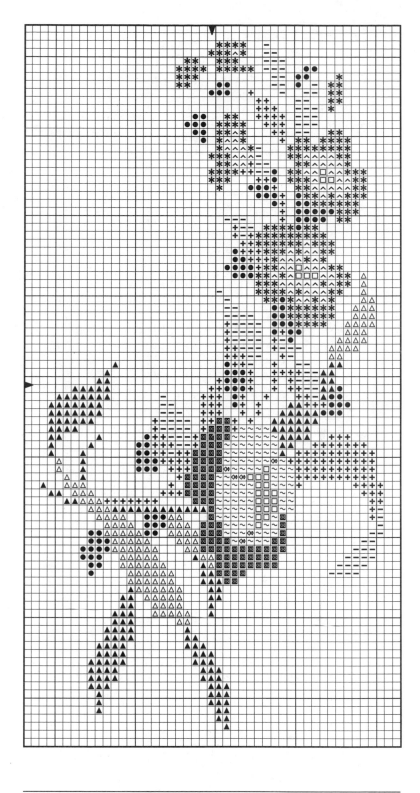

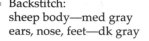

64 **Spring Sheep**
(57 wide x 12 high)

		Anchor	DMC
▫	= white	1	blanc
+	= pink	27	899
☆	= yellow	297	973
❖	= orange	324	721
◆	= blue	131	798
©	= purple	98	553
	med gray	235	414
■	= dk gray	401	413
│	= Backstitch:		

sheep body—med gray
ears, nose, feet—dk gray

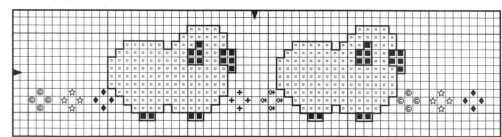

65 Pink Bow Teddy
(26 wide x 29 high)

		Anchor	DMC
□	= lt pink	26	894
+	= med pink	41	956
✖	= dk pink	42	326
◇	= tan	366	951
~	= lt brown	368	437
©	= dk brown	371	434
■	= black	403	310
|	= Backstitch: black		

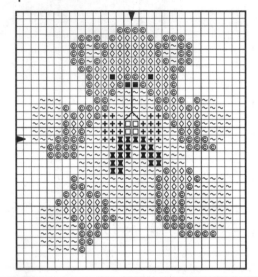

66 Green Bow Teddy
(26 wide x 29 high)

		Anchor	DMC
▫	= lt green	241	966
△	= med green	244	702
✖	= dk green	246	986
◇	= tan	366	951
~	= lt brown	368	437
©	= dk brown	371	434
■	= black	403	310
|	= Backstitch: black		

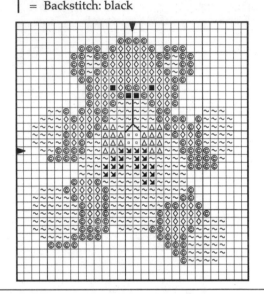

67 Ewe All Come Back
(23 wide x 31 high)

		Anchor	DMC
▫	= white	1	blanc
+	= pink	42	326
O	= yellow	305	743
◇	= green	246	986
■	= black	403	310
•	= French Knots: pink		
|	= Backstitch:		
	lettering—green		
	lamb—black		

68 Little Lamb
(30 wide x 30 high)

		Anchor	DMC
~	= white	1	blanc
✖	= pink	27	899
▲	= green	243	703
☆	= gray	399	318
■	= black	403	310
|	= Backstitch: gray		

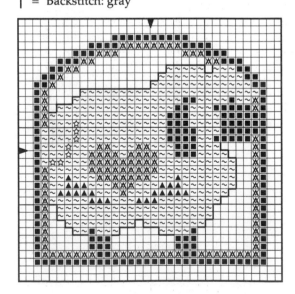

69 Les Petites Fleurs
(48 wide x 25 high)

		Anchor	DMC
□ =	yellow	297	973
⊞ =	gold	307	783
⊙ =	very lt green	265	3348
△ =	lt green	266	3347
✕ =	med green	257	905
■ =	dk green	268	469
— =	lt blue-green	185	964
⁄ =	med blue-green	186	959
◆ =	dk blue-green	187	958
▽ =	purple	96	3609

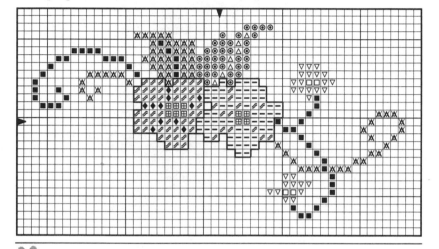

70 Tulip
(16 wide x 11 high)

		Anchor	DMC
✺ =	pink	42	326
△ =	lt green	241	704
▲ =	dk green	245	986
│ =	Backstitch: dk green		

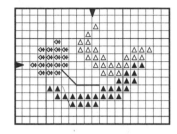

71 Woodland Spring

(41 wide x 30 high)

		Anchor	DMC
~ =	cream	386	746
✺ =	lt pink	36	3326
▨ =	dk pink	77	3687
▫ =	lt yellow	293	727
ω =	med yellow	305	743
✳ =	dk yellow	307	783
△ =	lt green	214	368
+ =	med green	216	502
▲ =	dk green	218	500
│ =	Backstitch: dk pink		

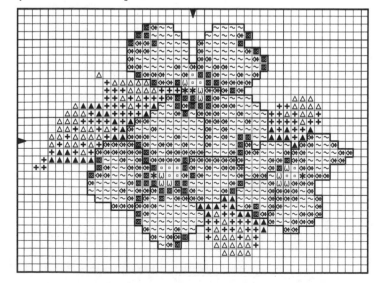

72 Home Sweet Home
(26 wide x 26 high)

		Anchor	DMC
◇ =	pink	26	894
◆ =	red	29	309
✺ =	orange	328	3341
▫ =	yellow	295	726
⊙ =	green	265	3347
☆ =	lt blue	130	809
★ =	med blue	131	798
+ =	purple	110	208
• =	French Knots: red		
│ =	Backstitch:		

stems, bottom "Home"—green
top "Home"—lt blue
"Sweet"—med blue

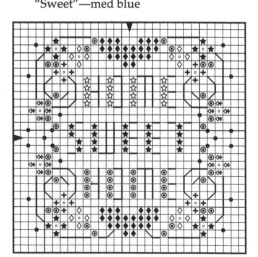

73 Spring Solo
(25 wide x 51 high)

		Anchor	DMC
□	= white	1	blanc
O	= lt orange	8	3824
×	= med orange	10	351
●	= dk orange	13	347
~	= yellow-green	255	907
◇	= lt green	1043	369
#	= med green	225	702
♦	= dk green	227	701
■	= very dk green	923	3818
	black	403	310

◊ = Lazy Daisies: black
| = Backstitch:
   petals—dk orange
   flower veins—yellow-green
   left leaf vein—lt green
   right leaf stem & vein—very dk green

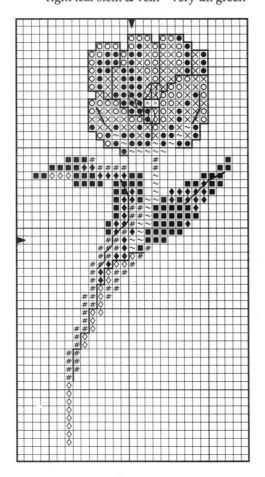

74 Nodding Tulip
(40 wide x 27 high)

		Anchor	DMC
×	= pink	40	335
●	= red	42	326
O	= yellow	298	972
+	= med green	877	501
▲	= dk green	879	500
|	= Backstitch: dk green		

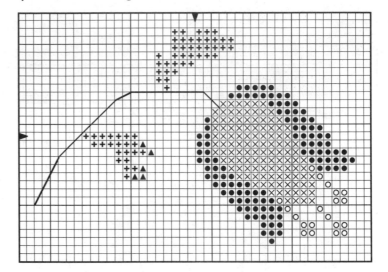

75 Elegant Iris
(48 wide x 38 high)

		Anchor	DMC
♡	= yellow	295	726
△	= lt green	241	966
#	= med green	244	702
~	= lt purple	342	211
❖	= med purple	110	208
■	= dk purple	112	552

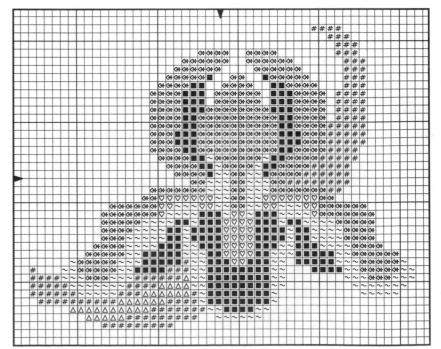

76 I Love You, Mom
(27 wide x 28 high)

		Anchor	DMC
♡	= pink	50	605
✿	= fuchsia	62	3806
+	= turquoise	186	959
▲	= blue	131	798

77 Baby Buggy
(27 wide x 31 high)

		Anchor	DMC
□	= white	1	blanc
✿	= pink	50	605
☆	= yellow	295	726
∿	= turquoise	185	964
✻	= blue	130	809
◇	= med gray	235	414
■	= dk gray	401	413

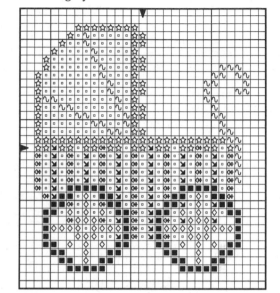

78 Welcome
(28 wide x 28 high)

		Anchor	DMC
□	= lt pink	24	963
◉	= med pink	40	956
+	= dk pink	28	892
	very dk pink	42	326
▽	= lt green	238	703
	dk green	245	986
☆	= lt blue	130	809
●	= med blue	132	797
✻	= brown	358	801
│	= Backstitch:		
	lettering—very dk pink		
	border lines—dk green		

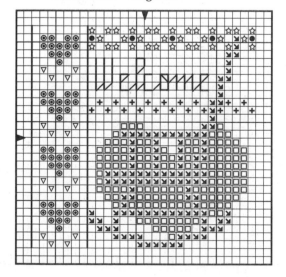

79 Baby Bird
(27 wide x 27 high)

		Anchor	DMC
▦	= red	13	347
✿	= med peach	9	352
✻	= dk peach	10	351
∿	= lt green	254	3348
+	= med green	238	703
✕	= dk green	245	986
∧	= lt blue	976	3752
★	= dk blue	978	312
✎	= rust	339	920
✕	= brown	369	435
■	= black	403	310

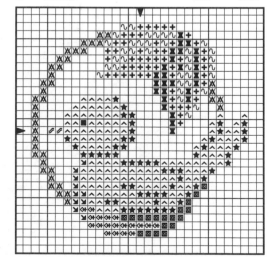

80 Butterfly & Bows

(34-wide repeat x 15 high)

		Anchor	DMC
	pink	63	3804
△	= med orange	323	3825
	dk orange	326	720
☆	= lt yellow	295	726
★	= med yellow	306	783
∧	= lt yellow-green	253	472
×	= med yellow-green	255	907
◇	= lt green	1043	369
#	= med green	241	966
◆	= dk green	244	702
✎	= lt blue-green	213	504
✎	= med blue-green	216	502
	dk blue-green	683	500

		Anchor	DMC
O	= lt blue	9159	828
⊙	= med blue	977	3755
●	= dk blue	979	312
~	= tan	933	543
⊞	= med brown	379	840
■	= dk brown	360	898
•	= French Knots:		
	scattered—dk orange		
	butterfly & antennae—dk brown		
|	= Backstitch:		
	ribbon—pink		
	leaf veins, stems—dk blue-green		
	butterfly—dk brown		

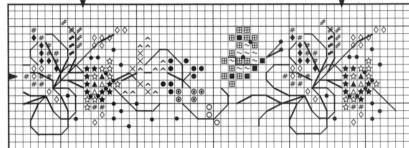

81 Rose Garden

(70 wide x 37 high)

		Anchor	DMC
~	= white	1	blanc
O	= very lt pink	48	3689
⊥	= lt pink	50	605
⊕	= med pink	40	956
#	= dk pink	59	326
▲	= red	44	815
∧	= lt peach	9	352
❂	= med peach	11	351

		Anchor	DMC
▫	= lt yellow	293	727
☆	= med yellow	306	725
◆	= gold	307	783
△	= lt green	254	3348
+	= med green	256	704
✔	= dk green	238	703
■	= very dk green	245	986
✎	= rust	1014	355
	gray	401	413
✳	= French Knots: rust		
•	= French Knots: gray		

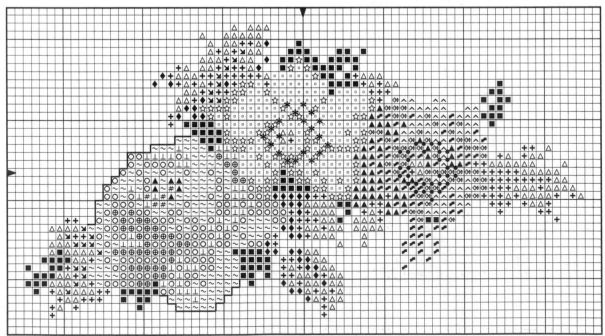

82 Baby Bluebird
(36 wide x 43 high)

		Anchor	DMC
▫	= white	1	blanc
∞	= pink	25	3716
☆	= orange	329	3340
□	= yellow	295	726
▣	= gold	298	972
▲	= green	244	702
◇	= lt blue	130	809
#	= med blue	131	798
■	= dk blue	132	797
O	= lt purple	96	3609
⊕	= med purple	99	552
●	= dk purple	101	550
		= Backstitch:		

white feathers—lt blue
beak, blue feathers—dk blue

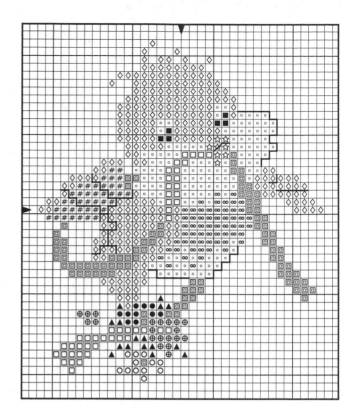

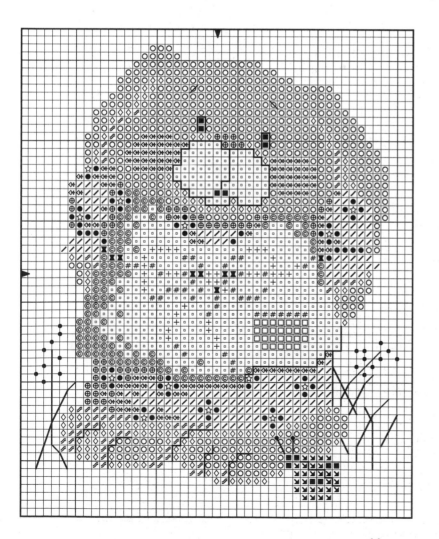

83 Bunny Friend
(45 wide x 57 high)

		Anchor	DMC
▫	= white	1	blanc
╱	= very lt pink	48	818
✼	= lt pink	25	3326
⊕	= med pink	41	956
●	= dk pink	59	326
✕	= red	47	321
☆	= yellow	293	727
□	= very lt green	240	368
+	= lt green	244	987
#	= med green	246	986
✕	= dk green	879	500
O	= tan	942	738
◇	= lt brown	363	436
╱	= med brown	310	434
✕	= dk brown	382	3371
©	= lt gray	399	318
	dk gray	235	414
■	= black	403	310
•	= French Knots:		

flowers—red (3 strands)
antennae—black

| = Backstitch:
dress—lt pink
stems, grass—med green
muzzle—med brown
feet, eyes, eyebrows—dk brown
apron—dk gray
ladybug—black

84 Daffodils
(23 wide x 46 high)

		Anchor	DMC
~	= lt yellow	292	3078
☆	= med yellow	288	445
★	= dk yellow	298	972
	very dk yellow	307	783
◇	= lt green	253	472
#	= med green	255	907
◆	= dk green	269	936
|	= Backstitch:		

flower centers—very dk
yellow
remaining outlines—dk yellow

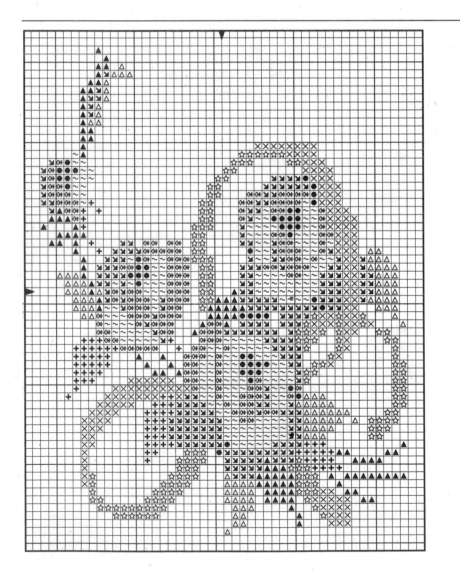

85 Beribboned Roses
(46 wide x 61 high)

		Anchor	DMC
~	= lt pink	24	963
✿	= med pink	27	899
➤	= dk pink	28	892
●	= very dk pink	59	326
△	= lt green	241	966
+	= med green	244	702
▲	= dk green	228	700
×	= lt blue	161	813
☆	= med blue	979	312

86 Folk Art Fancy
(41 wide x 23 high)

		Anchor	DMC
✿	= pink	26	894
⋈	= red	47	321
☆	= yellow	305	743
+	= lt green	209	913
✕	= dk green	212	561
▢	= blue	978	312

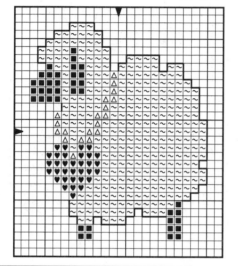

87 Lovey Lamb
(22 wide x 27 high)

		Anchor	DMC
♥	= pink	35	3801
△	= green	265	3347
~	= tan	885	739
■	= gray	401	413
		= Backstitch: gray	

88 Violets & Poppies
(48 wide x 53 high)

		Anchor	DMC
▫	= very lt pink	48	818
◇	= lt pink	26	894
✿	= med pink	28	892
◆	= dk pink	29	309
⊕	= fuchsia	86	3608
☆	= yellow	295	726
○	= lt yellow-green	254	3348
▲	= med yellow-green	256	704
⋇	= med green	244	702
⊞	= dk green	246	986
−	= lt purple	108	210
+	= med purple	110	208
●	= dk purple	101	550
		= Backstitch: dk green	

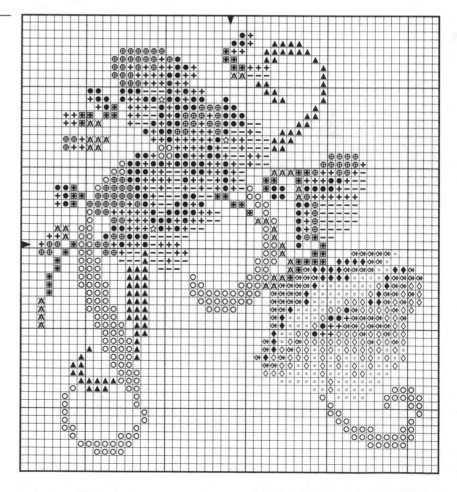

43

89 Pretty Posy

(20 wide x 14 high)

	Anchor	DMC
⊡ = yellow	305	743
⊞ = gold	307	783
⊙ = lt green	254	3348
◈ = med green	266	3347
■ = dk green	268	469
⊕ = rust	339	920
✱ = brown	352	300
| = Backstitch: gold		

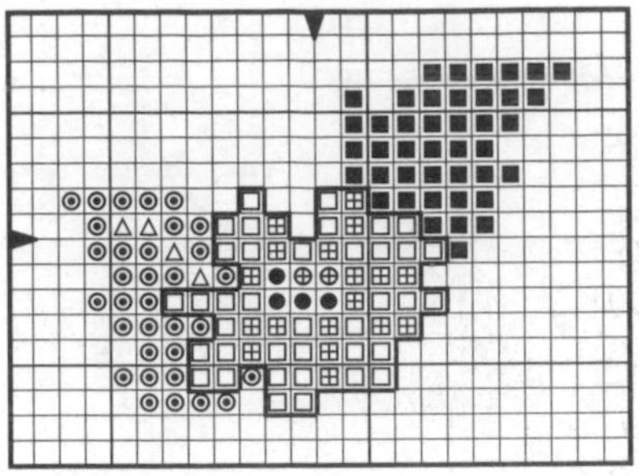

90 Spring Alphabet

	Anchor	DMC
▫ = pink	25	3326
↘ = red	47	321
− = lt orange	323	3825
Ӿ = dk orange	330	947
□ = yellow	295	726
★ = gold	307	783
○ = lt green	256	704
▲ = dk green	245	986
◇ = lt blue	130	809
● = dk blue	132	797
△ = lt purple	96	3609
⧖ = dk purple	100	327
+ = lt violet	109	209
◆ = dk violet	112	552
| = Backstitch: dk green		

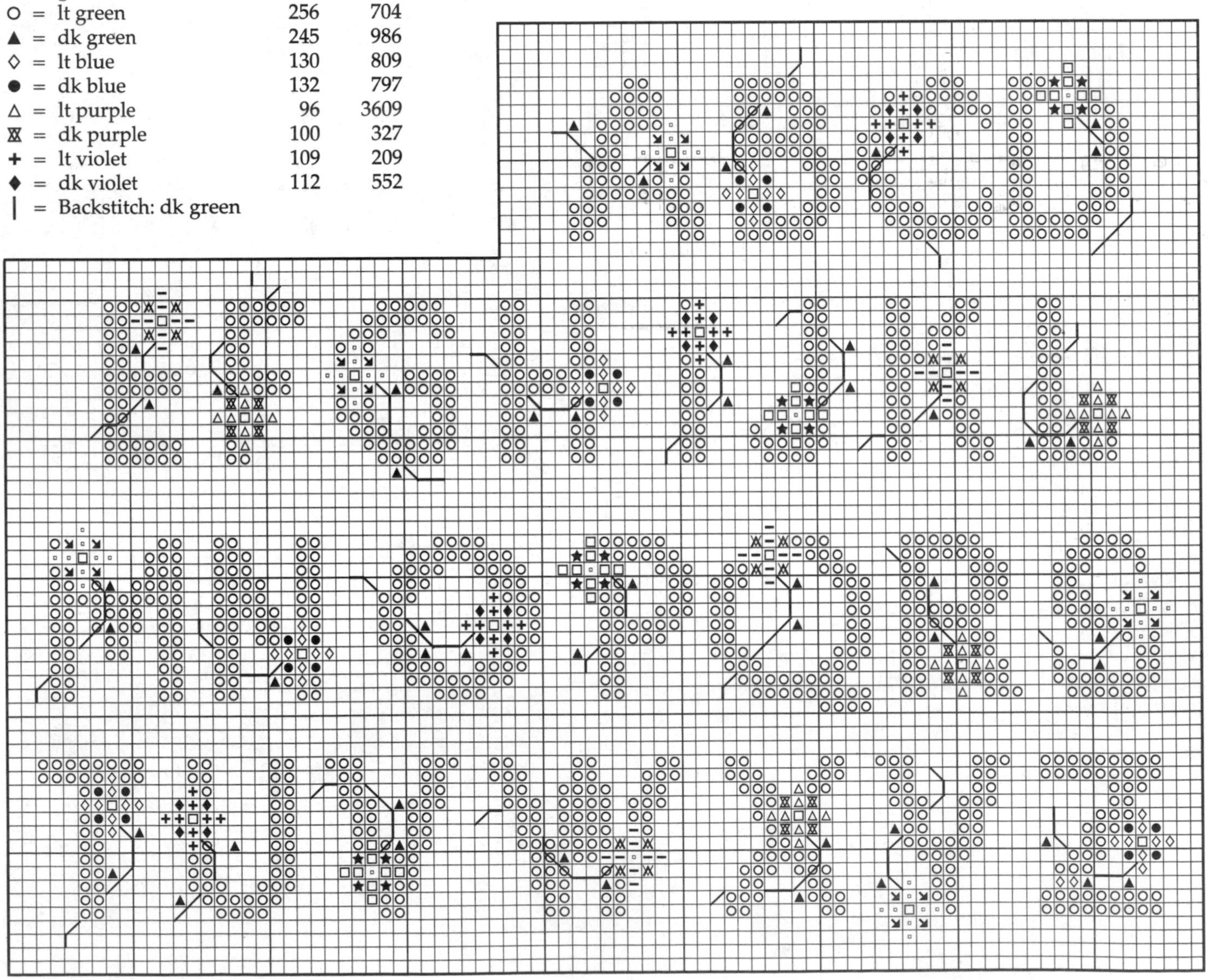

Summer

Summer

A TO Z

SNIPS AND SNAILS

SUGAR AND SPICE

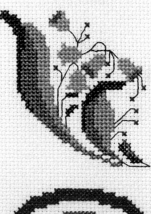

47

Summer

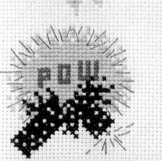

Flowers that fly

I'D RATHER BE
GOLFING

I'D RATHER
BE FISHING

Summer Design Directory

The charts are in numerical order beginning on page 50.

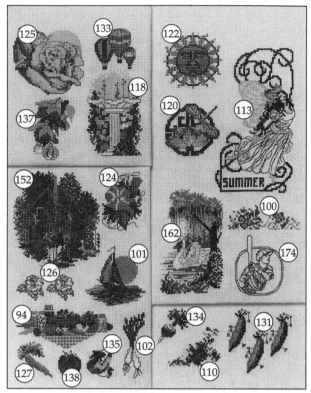

page 45

page 46

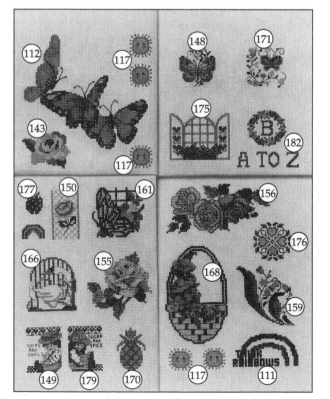

page 47

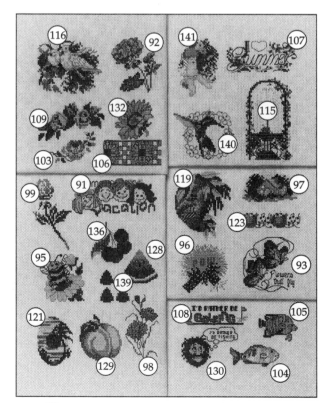

page 48

91 Summer Vacation
(58 wide x 25 high)

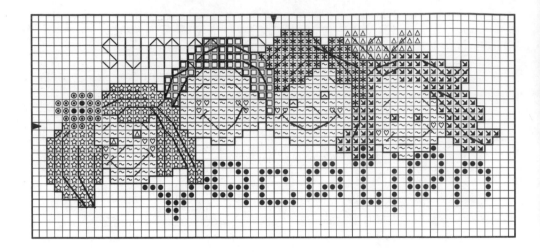

		Anchor	DMC
♡	= lt pink	23	3713
⊙	= med pink	31	3708
●	= red-orange	335	606
~	= peach	1011	948
✳	= orange	323	3825
☆	= yellow	305	743
	green	923	3818
△	= lt turquoise	928	3811
	dk turquoise	169	806
☐	= lt brown	368	437
⌃	= med brown	358	433
⋈	= dk brown	359	801
	very dk brown	382	3371
	rust	371	434

| = Backstitch:
"Summer"—green (2 strands)
turquoise bow—dk turquoise
faces, hair on two middle heads—dk brown
hair on fourth head—very dk brown
hair on first head—rust

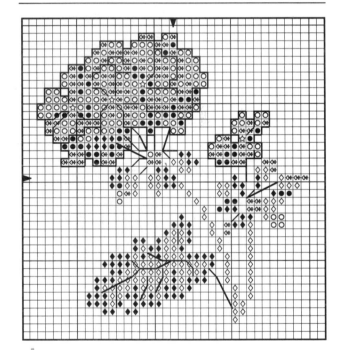

92 Geranium
(35 wide x 37 high)

		Anchor	DMC
○	= lt red	1021	761
✪	= med red	1023	3712
●	= dk red	29	309
☆	= yellow	297	973
◇	= lt green	261	989
◆	= dk green	263	3362

| = Backstitch:
flowers—dk red
stems, leaf—dk green

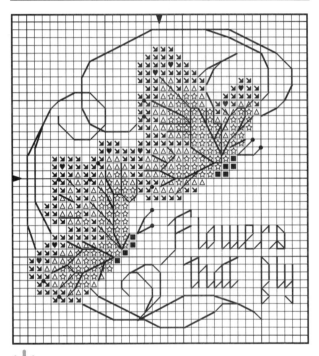

93 Flowers That Fly
(34 wide x 38 high)

		Anchor	DMC
♥	= red	334	606
△	= orange	1003	922
☆	= yellow	295	726
	green	229	910
⋈	= brown	371	434
■	= gray	400	317
•	= French Knots:		
	butterflies—red		
	antennae—gray		

| = Backstitch:
tracery—green
lettering—brown
wings, antennae—gray

94 **Salad Days** (64 wide x 29 high)

		Anchor	DMC				Anchor	DMC			Anchor	DMC
▫	= white	1	blanc	◇	=	lt green	1043	369		dk gray	236	3799
○	= lt red	1024	3328	◆	=	dk green	1044	895	• = French Knots: dk gray			
●	= dk red	47	321	♡	=	lt blue-green	215	320	❘ = Backstitch:			
✥	= lt orange	323	3825	♥	=	dk blue-green	218	319	orange jar—dk orange			
■	= dk orange	332	946	△	=	lt blue-gray	848	927	green jar—dk green			
☆	= yellow	288	445	▲	=	dk blue-gray	850	926	green pepper—dk blue-green			
+	= med yellow-green	265	3347	^	=	lt gray	398	415	red jar, yellow jar, jar lids—med gray			
✎	= dk yellow-green	269	936	✕	=	med gray	235	414	colander—dk gray			

95 **Sitting Pretty** (30 wide x 32 high)

		Anchor	DMC
~	= lt pink	24	963
	dk pink	27	899
☆	= yellow	290	973
◇	= lt green	257	905
	dk green	268	469
△	= med brown	358	801
▲	= dk brown	380	838
	gray	400	317
■	= black	403	310
❘	= Backstitch:		

petals—dk pink
stem, leaves—dk green
wings—gray
eyes, head, antennae, mouth,
legs, stinger—black

96 **POW!** (34 wide x 34 high)

		Anchor	DMC
▫	= white	1	blanc
	red	9046	666
●	= orange	316	970
☆	= yellow	305	743
▲	= blue	134	820
^	= gray	235	414
❘	= Backstitch:		

firecracker cases—red
\ = Straight Stitches:
explosion lines—orange

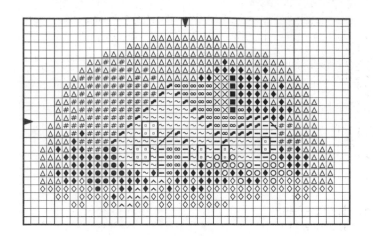

Country Cottage
(37 wide x 22 high)

			Anchor	DMC
▫	=	white	1	blanc
−	=	lt cream	885	739
~	=	med cream	372	738
○	=	lt rose	894	223
●	=	dk rose	897	221
◇	=	lt green	240	966
#	=	med green	229	910
◆	=	dk green	1044	895
△	=	blue	1037	3756
∞	=	lt blue-gray	1032	3752
✔	=	med blue-gray	1034	931
^	=	brown	358	801
×	=	med rust	1013	3778
■	=	dk rust	1014	355
|	=	Backstitch: med blue-gray		

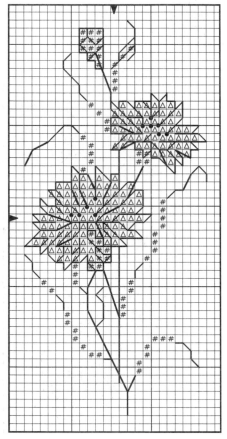

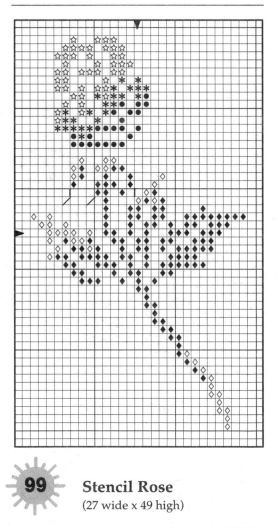

 **98**

Cornflowers
(23 wide x 49 high)

			Anchor	DMC
		yellow	290	973
#	=	med green	242	989
		dk green	244	702
△	=	lt blue	140	3755
		dk blue	143	797
•	=	French Knots: yellow		
|	=	Backstitch:		
		stems—dk green		
		flowers—dk blue		

99

Stencil Rose
(27 wide x 49 high)

			Anchor	DMC
●	=	red	335	606
✳	=	orange	329	3340
☆	=	yellow	303	742
◇	=	lt green	241	966
◆	=	dk green	246	986
|	=	Backstitch: dk green		

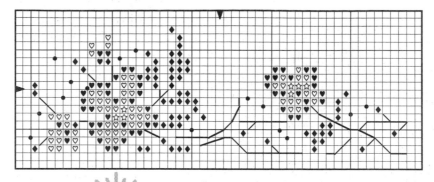

100 Purple Posies
(47 wide x 16 high)

		Anchor	DMC
☆ =	yellow	291	444
◆ =	green	243	703
♡ =	lt purple	96	3609
♥ =	dk purple	100	327
• =	French Knots: dk purple		
| =	Backstitch: green		

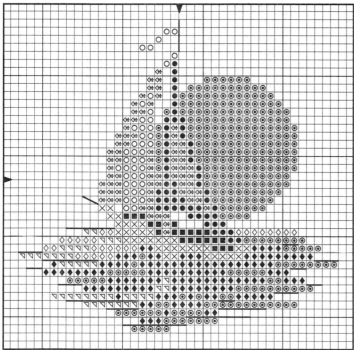

101 Sails At Sunset
(40 wide x 39 high)

		Anchor	DMC
○ =	lt red	1022	760
✿ =	med red	1024	3328
● =	dk red	1015	3777
◸ =	lt orange	313	742
◉ =	dk orange	314	741
◇ =	lt green	875	3813
◆ =	dk green	879	500
✕ =	med brown	359	801
■ =	dk brown	380	838
| =	Backstitch:		
	water—dk green		
	boat—dk brown		

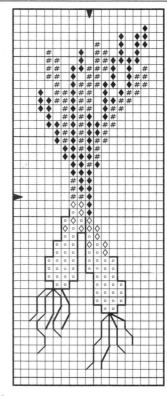

102 Onions
(15 wide x 43 high)

		Anchor	DMC
▫ =	white	1	blanc
◇ =	lt green	213	504
# =	med green	216	502
◆ =	dk green	218	319
	brown	357	433
| =	Backstitch: brown		

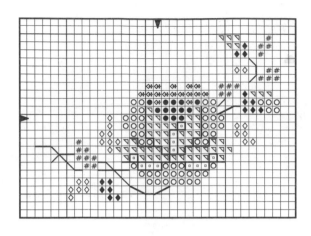

103 Pink Posy
(31 wide x 21 high)

		Anchor	DMC
▫ =	white	1	blanc
◿ =	very lt peach	6	754
○ =	lt peach	9	352
✥ =	med peach	11	351
● =	dk peach	13	347
◇ =	lt green	241	966
# =	med green	243	703
◆ =	dk green	246	986
| =	Backstitch:		

rose—dk peach
stems—dk green

104 Tropical Swimmer
(33 wide x 15 high)

		Anchor	DMC
▫ =	white	1	blanc
☆ =	yellow	289	307
◆ =	green	228	700
△ =	lt turquoise	1038	519
▲ =	dk turquoise	433	996
	gray	400	317
■ =	black	403	310
| =	Backstitch:		

yellow & white areas—lt turquoise
middle back fins—black
remaining—gray

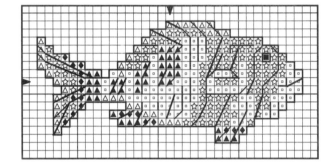

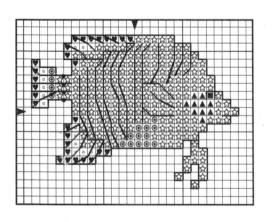

105 Angel Fish
(26 wide x 19 high)

		Anchor	DMC
▫ =	white	1	blanc
◉ =	med red	9046	321
♥ =	dk red	22	814
☆ =	yellow	291	444
▲ =	turquoise	433	996
	gray	400	317
■ =	black	403	310
• =	French Knots: gray		
| =	Backstitch:		

long vertical body stripes—med red
remaining—gray

106 Checkerboard Mums
(24-wide repeat x 17 high)

		Anchor	DMC
− =	yellow	297	973
◇ =	green	243	703
△ =	lt blue	1033	932
	dk blue	1035	930
^ =	med brown	358	801
◉ =	dk brown	380	838
■ =	very dk brown	382	3371
| =	Backstitch:		

checkerboard—dk blue
flower—dk brown

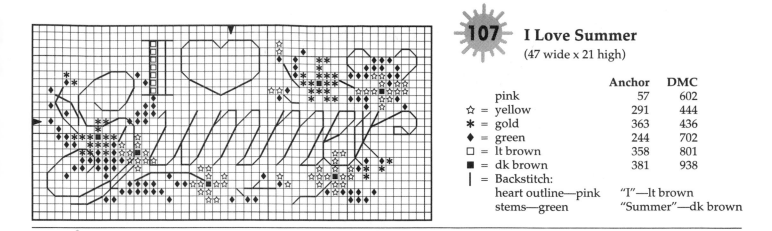

107 I Love Summer

(47 wide x 21 high)

		Anchor	DMC
	pink	57	602
☆ =	yellow	291	444
✶ =	gold	363	436
◆ =	green	244	702
☐ =	lt brown	358	801
■ =	dk brown	381	938
| =	Backstitch:		

heart outline—pink   "I"—lt brown
stems—green   "Summer"—dk brown

108 I'd Rather Be Golfing

(43 wide x 13 high)

		Anchor	DMC
☆ =	yellow	291	444
◇ =	lt yellow-green	253	472
◆ =	dk yellow-green	268	469
# =	med green	225	702
	dk green	228	700
∧ =	brown	370	434
✕ =	lt gray	398	415
■ =	dk gray	400	317
| =	Backstitch:		

"I'D RATHER BE"—dk yellow-green
"Golfing"—dk green
club, flag, pole—dk gray

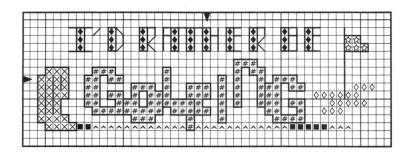

110 Mixed Bouquet

(34 wide x 24 high)

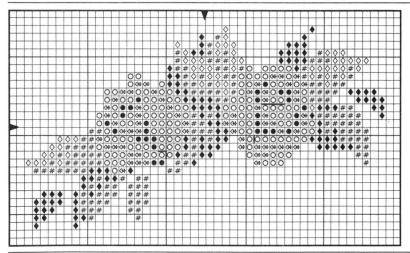

		Anchor	DMC
● =	red	335	606
✶ =	orange	329	3340
☆ =	yellow	298	972
◇ =	lt green	239	702
◆ =	dk green	228	700
♥ =	purple	94	917
♡ =	brown	1049	3826

109 Posy Pair

(46 wide x 26 high)

		Anchor	DMC
○ =	lt rose	74	3354
✻ =	med rose	76	961
● =	dk rose	65	3685
◇ =	lt green	240	966
# =	med green	244	702
◆ =	dk green	1044	895
| =	Backstitch: dk rose		

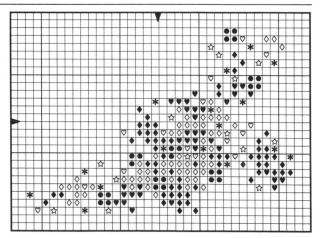

111 Think Rainbows
(44 wide x 22 high)

		Anchor	DMC
✤	= red	29	309
+	= blue	137	798
■	= blue-black	127	939

112 Butterflies In Flight
(82 wide x 75 high)

		Anchor	DMC
~	= pink	40	956
◇	= gold	295	726
△	= lt blue	130	809
+	= med blue	131	798
▲	= dk blue	132	797
✤	= purple	99	552
▫	= lt brown	368	437
●	= med brown	371	434
■	= dk brown	381	938
•	= French Knots: dk brown		
|	= Backstitch: dk brown		

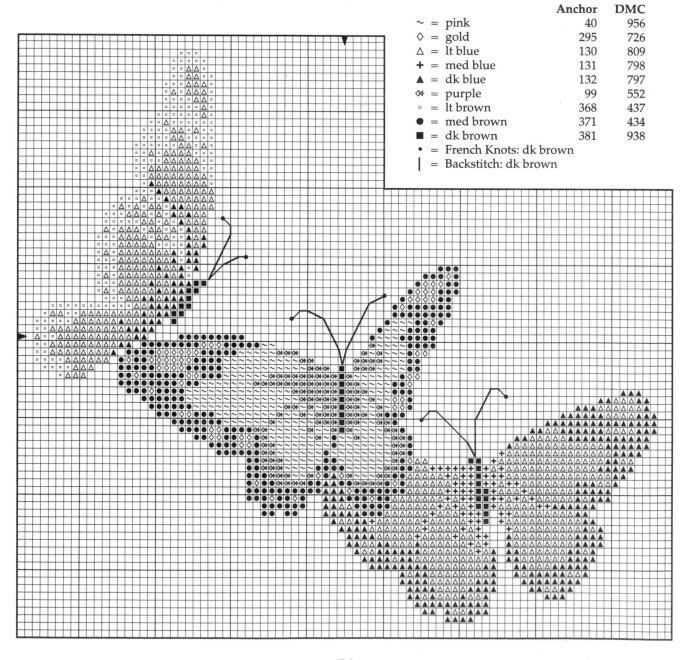

113 Summer Fairy
(52 wide x 95 high)

Note: For wings, use two strands of floss and one strand of pearl (032) blending filament.

			Anchor	DMC
▫	=	white / filament	1 / 032	blanc / 032
∞	=	lt pink /	271 /	819 /
		filament	032	032
		dk pink	63	3804
~	=	lt peach	1011	948
◈	=	med peach	1012	754
		dk peach	9	352
—	=	very lt yellow /	293 /	727 /
		filament	032	032
☆	=	med yellow	305	743
★	=	dk yellow	890	729
✔	=	lt yellow-green /	259 /	772 /
		filament	032	032
◢	=	dk yellow-green	262	3363
◆	=	green	229	910
◄	=	very lt blue /	1031 /	3753 /
		filament	032	032
∧	=	med brown	371	434
⋈	=	dk brown	359	801
		very dk brown	380	838

- • = French Knot: very dk brown
- ⎮ = Backstitch:
  sash—dk pink
  hands, feet—dk peach
  dress—green
  eyes, mouth, edge of face—very dk
    brown

114 Mini Rainbow
(15 wide x 9 high)

			Anchor	DMC
★	=	orange	328	3341
✕	=	yellow	305	743
⋈	=	blue	137	798
+	=	purple	98	553

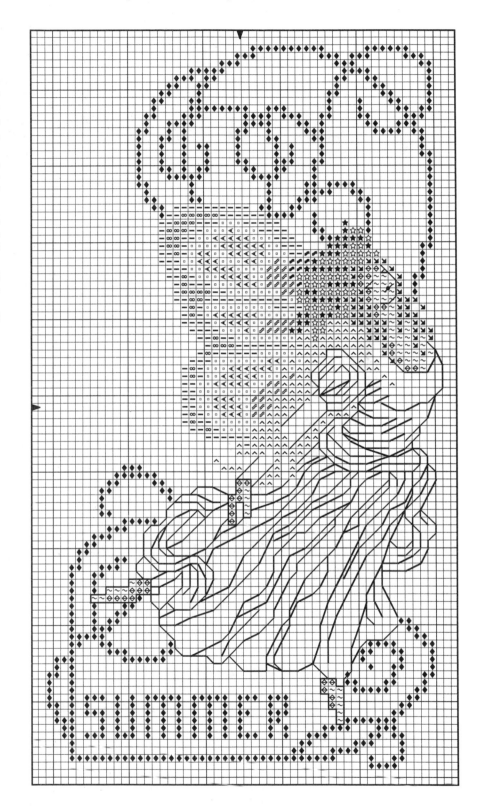

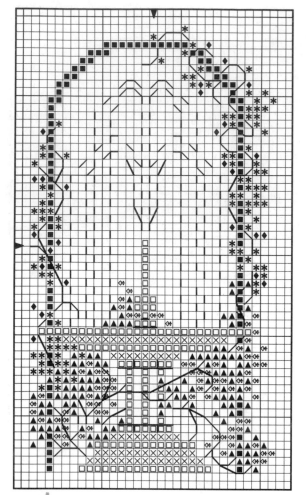

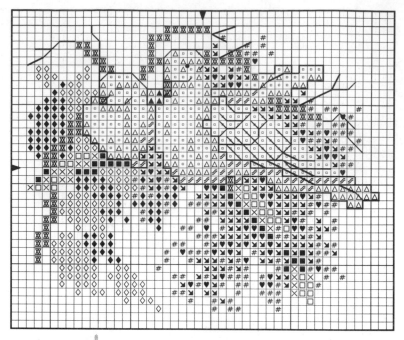

Turtle Doves
(44 wide x 36 high)

		Anchor	DMC
▫	= white	1	blanc
♥	= red	29	309
#	= med green	242	989
✔	= dk green	1044	895
◇	= lt gray-green	858	524
◆	= dk gray-green	860	522
△	= lt blue	9159	828
✎	= med blue	1038	519
▲	= dk blue	1039	518
□	= lt brown	933	543
×	= med brown	378	841
■	= dk brown	936	632
⊠	= med gray	400	317
	dk gray	236	3799
•	= French Knot: dk gray		
|	= Backstitch:		
	birds—dk blue		
	branches—med gray		
	beaks, eyes—dk gray		

Fountain
(31 wide x 56 high)

		Anchor	DMC
❖	= pink	26	894
✳	= orange	330	947
◆	= green	243	703
▲	= med blue-green	877	3815
	dk blue-green	879	500
	blue	159	3325
□	= lt brown	369	435
×	= med brown	371	434
■	= dk brown	352	300
|	= Backstitch:		
	vertical vines—green		
	vines below fountain—dk blue-green		
	water—blue		
	fountain—dk brown		

Happy Sun
(13 wide x 13 high)

		Anchor	DMC
★	= yellow-orange	303	742
	orange	304	741
○	= yellow	297	973
■	= gray	236	3799
•	= French Knots: orange		
|	= Backstitch: orange		

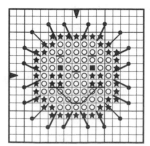

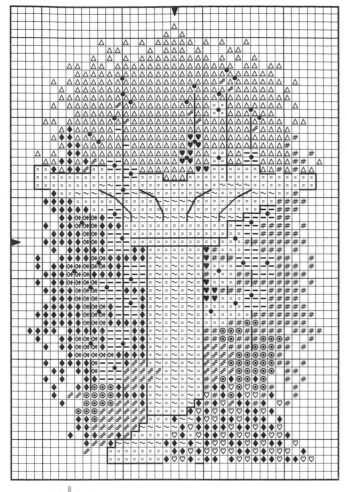

 118 Birdbath

(37 wide x 55 high)

			Anchor	DMC
□	=	white	1	blanc
—	=	lt pink	24	963
✿	=	med pink	26	894
♥	=	dk pink	28	892
		yellow	297	973
⌇	=	lt yellow-green	260	772
◉	=	med yellow-green	262	3363
		dk yellow-green	269	936
#	=	med green	227	701
◆	=	dk green	1044	895
△	=	blue	1031	3753
♡	=	purple	109	209
~	=	lt gray	398	415
		med gray	400	317

• = French Knots:
  hollyhock centers—yellow
  buds on stems—dk yellow-green
| = Backstitch:
  stems—dk yellow-green
  birdbath—med gray

119 Early Bird

(38 wide x 48 high)

			Anchor	DMC
		white	1	blanc
~	=	cream	366	951
○	=	lt orange	313	742
∞	=	med orange	1003	922
●	=	dk orange	1004	920
◇	=	lt green	1043	369
#	=	med green	242	989
◆	=	dk green	1044	895
△	=	lt blue	9159	828
⊕	=	med blue	161	813
▲	=	dk blue	164	824
✖	=	brown	371	434
^	=	lt gray	398	415
✕	=	med gray	235	414
		dk gray	236	3799
■	=	black	403	310

• = French Knot: white
| = Backstitch:
  veins—med green
  eye—lt gray
  beak, feathers—dk gray

59

120 **Oriental Summer**
(34 wide x 34 high)

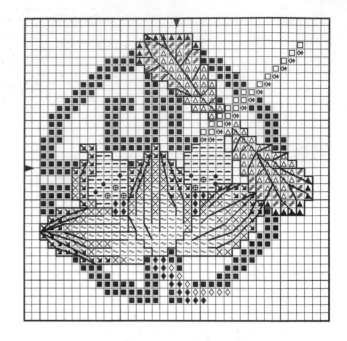

		Anchor	DMC
⊕ =	rose	970	3726
~ =	lt peach	1012	754
✕ =	med peach	6	761
⟐ =	dk peach	10	351
− =	yellow	293	727
◇ =	lt yellow-green	261	989
◆ =	dk yellow-green	263	3362
⚞ =	lt turquoise	185	964
▲ =	dk turquoise	188	3812
△ =	blue	158	747
▢ =	lt brown	376	3774
✧ =	med brown	379	840
■ =	dk brown	936	632
	gray	400	317
• =	French Knots: rose		
| =	Backstitch:		
	petals—dk peach		
	wings—gray		

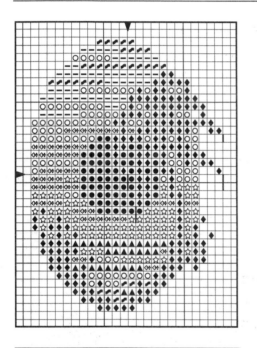

121 **Island Sunset**
(24 wide x 34 high)

		Anchor	DMC
○ =	pink	1020	3713
✧ =	lt red	1023	3712
● =	med red	1025	347
☆ =	yellow	293	727
◆ =	green	1044	895
▲ =	blue	137	798
− =	lt purple	342	211
⟋ =	med purple	110	208
| =	Backstitch: green		

 122 **Aztec Sun**
(37 wide x 37 high)

		Anchor	DMC
	white	1	blanc
∧ =	lt rust	347	402
✳ =	med rust	349	301
⟐ =	dk rust	352	300
▲ =	blue-gray	779	3809
• =	French Knots: white		
| =	Backstitch: dk rust		

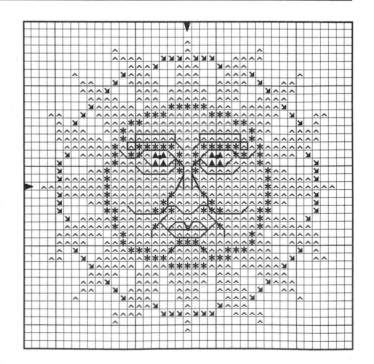

123 Birdsong (20-wide repeat x 10 high)

		Anchor	DMC
✧	= pink	38	961
	orange	316	970
◇	= green	244	702
△	= lt blue	144	800

		Anchor	DMC
▲	= dk blue	146	798
■	= gray	400	317
	black	403	310
•	= French Knots: black		

| = Backstitch:
  beaks—orange
  stems—green
  notes—gray

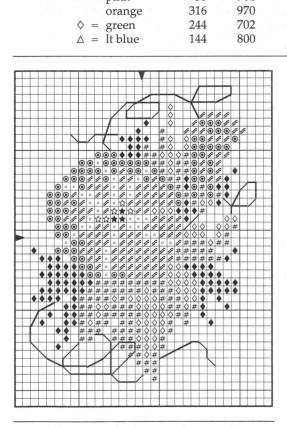

124 Morning Glory
(28 wide x 37 high)

		Anchor	DMC
▫	= white	1	blanc
☆	= med yellow	291	444
★	= dk yellow	307	783
◇	= lt yellow-green	265	3347
#	= med yellow-green	267	469
◆	= dk yellow-green	269	936
⊙	= blue	176	793
✐	= purple	109	209

| = Backstitch: med yellow-green

125 Grandiflora
(46 wide x 44 high)

		Anchor	DMC
∞	= very lt peach	1012	754
○	= lt peach	8	3824
⊕	= med peach	10	351
●	= dk peach	13	347
	very dk peach	11	3705
☆	= lt yellow	289	307
⊙	= med yellow	306	783
★	= dk yellow	308	781
◇	= lt green	259	772
#	= med green	261	989
◆	= dk green	263	3362

| = Backstitch: very dk peach

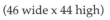

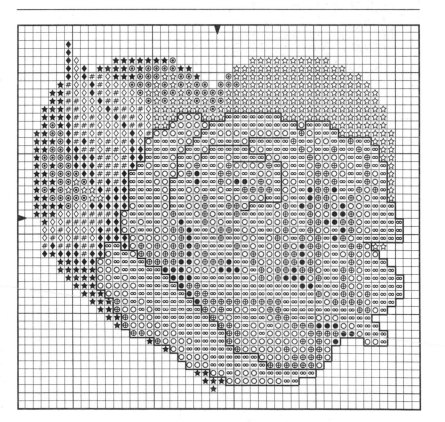

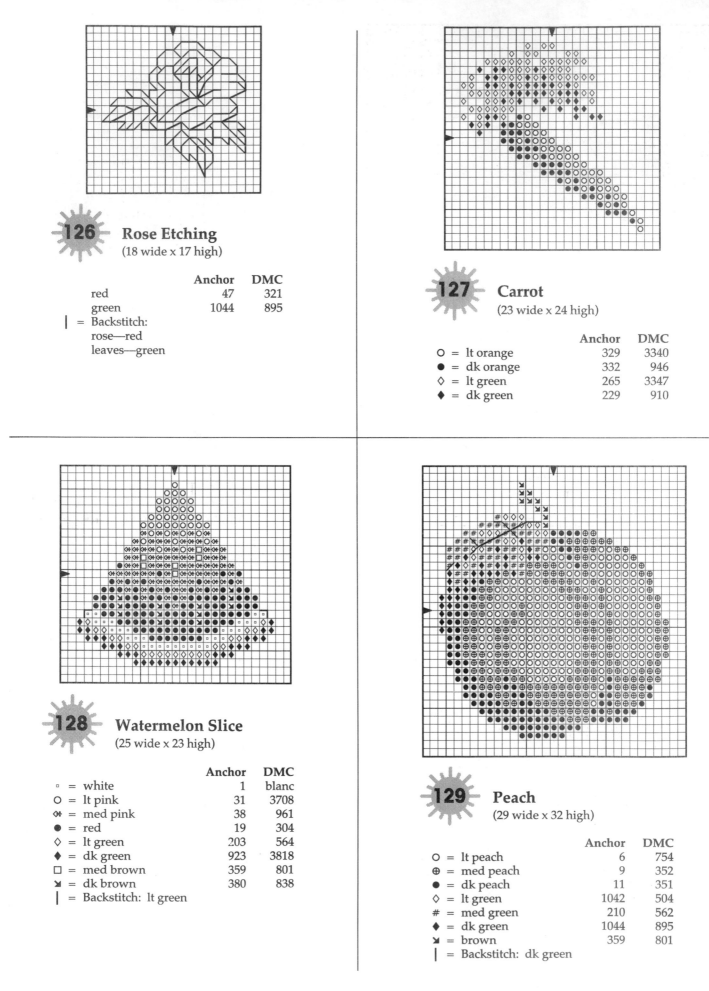

126 **Rose Etching**
(18 wide x 17 high)

	Anchor	DMC
red	47	321
green	1044	895

| = Backstitch:
rose—red
leaves—green

127 **Carrot**
(23 wide x 24 high)

		Anchor	DMC
○ =	lt orange	329	3340
● =	dk orange	332	946
◇ =	lt green	265	3347
◆ =	dk green	229	910

128 **Watermelon Slice**
(25 wide x 23 high)

		Anchor	DMC
▫ =	white	1	blanc
○ =	lt pink	31	3708
✷ =	med pink	38	961
● =	red	19	304
◇ =	lt green	203	564
◆ =	dk green	923	3818
□ =	med brown	359	801
⌦ =	dk brown	380	838

| = Backstitch: lt green

129 **Peach**
(29 wide x 32 high)

		Anchor	DMC
○ =	lt peach	6	754
⊕ =	med peach	9	352
● =	dk peach	11	351
◇ =	lt green	1042	504
# =	med green	210	562
◆ =	dk green	1044	895
⌦ =	brown	359	801

| = Backstitch: dk green

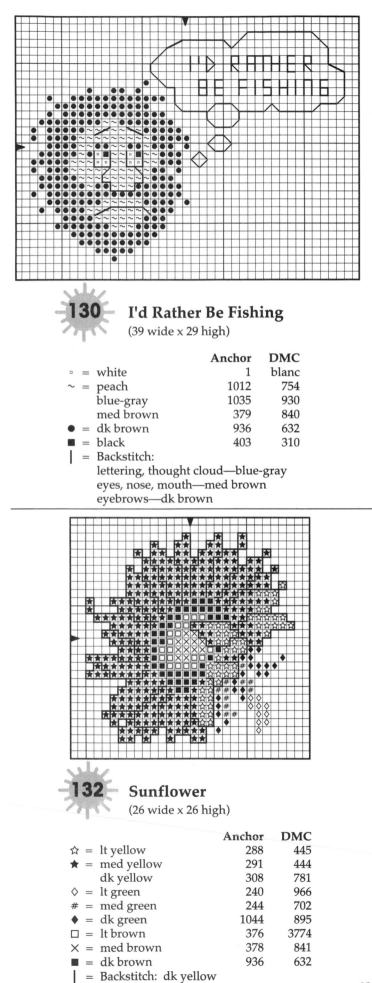
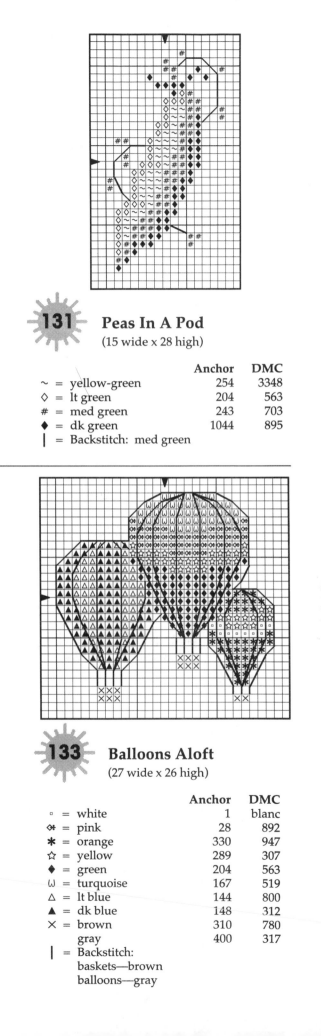

130 I'd Rather Be Fishing
(39 wide x 29 high)

		Anchor	DMC
▫	= white	1	blanc
~	= peach	1012	754
	blue-gray	1035	930
	med brown	379	840
●	= dk brown	936	632
■	= black	403	310
|	= Backstitch:		

lettering, thought cloud—blue-gray
eyes, nose, mouth—med brown
eyebrows—dk brown

131 Peas In A Pod
(15 wide x 28 high)

		Anchor	DMC
~	= yellow-green	254	3348
◇	= lt green	204	563
#	= med green	243	703
◆	= dk green	1044	895
|	= Backstitch: med green		

132 Sunflower
(26 wide x 26 high)

		Anchor	DMC
☆	= lt yellow	288	445
★	= med yellow	291	444
	dk yellow	308	781
◇	= lt green	240	966
#	= med green	244	702
◆	= dk green	1044	895
☐	= lt brown	376	3774
✕	= med brown	378	841
■	= dk brown	936	632
|	= Backstitch: dk yellow		

133 Balloons Aloft
(27 wide x 26 high)

		Anchor	DMC
▫	= white	1	blanc
✳	= pink	28	892
✳	= orange	330	947
☆	= yellow	289	307
◆	= green	204	563
ω	= turquoise	167	519
△	= lt blue	144	800
▲	= dk blue	148	312
✕	= brown	310	780
	gray	400	317
|	= Backstitch:		

baskets—brown
balloons—gray

63

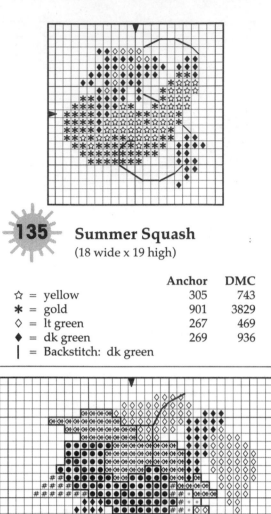

134 Radish
(22 wide x 23 high)

			Anchor	DMC
□	=	white	1	blanc
⋈	=	lt red	1023	3712
●	=	dk red	9046	321
◇	=	lt green	216	502
◆	=	dk green	923	3818
∣	=	Backstitch: lt red		

135 Summer Squash
(18 wide x 19 high)

			Anchor	DMC
☆	=	yellow	305	743
✳	=	gold	901	3829
◇	=	lt green	267	469
◆	=	dk green	269	936
∣	=	Backstitch: dk green		

137 Fuchsia
(31 wide x 40 high)

			Anchor	DMC
□	=	white	1	blanc
⋈	=	lt pink	55	957
		dk pink	57	602
◇	=	lt green	213	504
#	=	med green	215	320
◆	=	dk green	218	319
●	=	med purple	110	208
		dk purple	112	552
∣	=	Backstitch:		
		pink petals & buds—dk pink		
		calyxes, stem, leaf vein—dk green		
		purple petals—dk purple		

136 Cherries
(28 wide x 28 high)

			Anchor	DMC
⊕	=	med red	47	321
●	=	dk red	22	814
◇	=	lt green	1042	504
#	=	med green	205	912
◆	=	dk green	923	3818
∣	=	Backstitch:		
		stems—med green		
		veins—dk green		

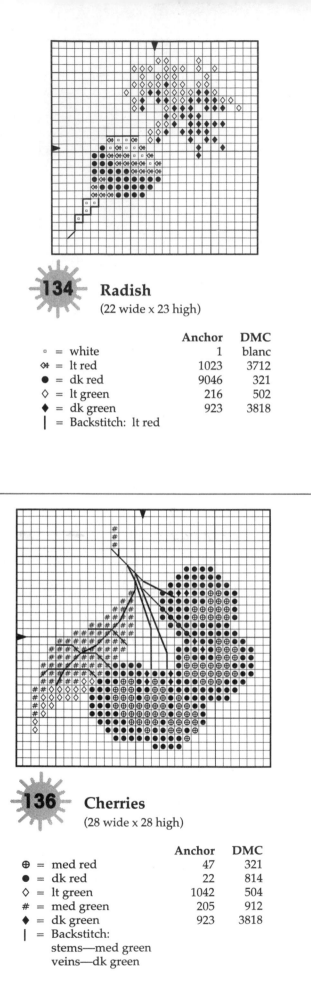

138 Tomato
(15 wide x 16 high)

		Anchor	DMC
○ =	lt red	35	3801
● =	dk red	46	666
◇ =	med green	242	989
◆ =	dk green	245	986
| =	Backstitch: dk green		

139 Watermelon Bites (12-wide repeat x 10 high)

		Anchor	DMC			Anchor	DMC
◉ =	red	19	304	⋈ =	brown	380	838
◆ =	green	923	3818				

140 Hummingbird
(41 wide x 35 high)

		Anchor	DMC
❖ =	pink	57	602
◇ =	lt yellow-green	842	3013
# =	med yellow-green	844	3012
◆ =	very dk yellow-green	846	3011
◣ =	green	246	986
~ =	very lt gray	234	762
∧ =	lt gray	399	318
✕ =	med gray	400	317
⊞ =	dk gray	236	3799
■ =	black	403	310
• =	French Knots: pink		
| =	Backstitch:		
	border—pink		
	eye—very lt gray		

141 Summer Cupid
(27 wide x 39 high)

		Anchor	DMC
▫ =	white	1	blanc
	pink	52	957
~ =	lt peach	1009	3770
◉ =	med peach	1012	754
☆ =	lt yellow	293	727
★ =	dk yellow	297	973
◇ =	lt yellow-green	266	3347
◆ =	dk yellow-green	269	936
# =	green	244	702
△ =	lt blue	120	3747
▲ =	dk blue	136	799
⋈ =	brown	370	434
○ =	lt rust	336	758
✱ =	dk rust	338	922
	gray	400	317
• =	French Knots:		
	in flowers—pink		
	mouth—gray		
| =	Backstitch:		
	ribbon, wings—dk blue		
	skin—lt rust eyes, mouth—gray		

142 Gazebo
(28 wide x 33 high)

		Anchor	DMC
▫	= white	1	blanc
+	= lt green	238	703
ω	= dk green	923	3818
✲	= lt blue-gray	117	341
✘	= dk blue-gray	177	792
●	= purple	110	208
	gray	235	414
|	= Backstitch: gray		

143 Summer Rose
(32 wide x 24 high)

		Anchor	DMC
~	= very lt rose	49	963
✲	= lt rose	55	957
◉	= med rose	54	956
✘	= dk rose	42	326
●	= very dk rose	1006	304
+	= lt green	209	913
▲	= dk green	245	986

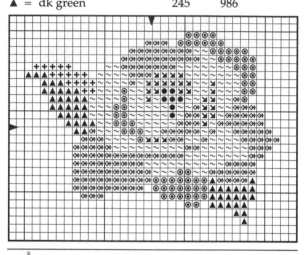

145 Rose & Forget-Me-Nots
(22 wide x 28 high)

		Anchor	DMC
▽	= lt pink	36	3326
◆	= med pink	41	956
■	= red	1006	304
▫	= yellow	295	726
	med green	238	703
+	= dk green	245	986
☆	= lt blue	130	809
	dk blue	132	797
	brown	371	434
•	= French Knots:		
	flower centers—yellow		
	flower dots—dk blue		
|	= Backstitch:		
	stems—med green flower petals—brown		

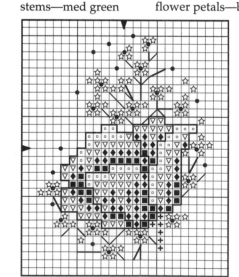

144 Rose Crescent
(43 wide x 20 high)

		Anchor	DMC
✲	= med rose	55	957
✘	= dk rose	57	602
∿	= orange	328	3341
O	= yellow	301	744
◇	= lt green	266	3347
▲	= dk green	257	905
■	= brown	370	434
	gray	236	3799
|	= Backstitch:		
	yellow & orange roses—brown		
	remaining roses, leaves—gray		

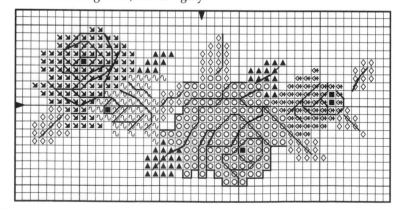

146 Home Sweet Home
(43 wide x 39 high)

		Anchor	DMC
▲	= med pink	895	223
■	= dk pink	896	3721
- - -	= Running Stitch: med pink		
|	= Backstitch: med pink		

147 Country Couple
(26 wide x 23 high)

		Anchor	DMC
−	= cream	276	739
◇	= lt pink	50	605
★	= dk pink	41	956
	red	29	309
▫	= peach	8	3824
✤	= yellow	307	783
✖	= green	258	905
☆	= lt blue	130	809
▲	= dk blue	137	798
○	= lt brown	362	437
●	= dk brown	5975	355
•	= French Knots:		
	apron dots—lt pink		
	eyes, mouths—dk brown		
|	= Backstitch:		
	outer heart outline—dk pink		
	tulip design on apron—red		
	apron decoration—green		
	hair, faces—lt brown		
	pants, hat—dk brown		

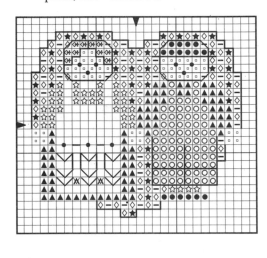

148 Majestic Butterfly
(24 wide x 26 high)

		Anchor	DMC
▫	= lt yellow	295	726
◆	= dk yellow	306	783
★	= orange	324	721
✤	= green	267	469
▽	= lt brown	369	435
■	= dk brown	357	433
•	= French Knots:		
	flowers—orange		
	antennae—dk brown		
|	= Backstitch:		
	stems—green		
	butterfly outline—lt brown		
	inside wing, antennae—dk brown		

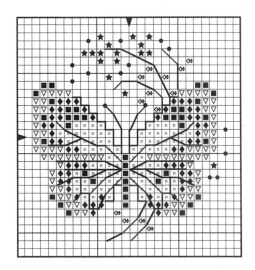

149 Snips And Snails
(24 wide x 30 high)

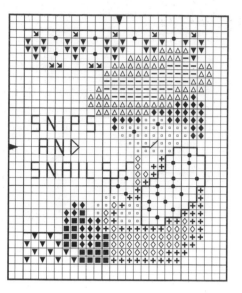

			Anchor	DMC
▼	=	red	47	304
▫	=	peach	8	3824
△	=	gold	306	783
⋈	=	green	266	3347
◇	=	lt blue	130	809
+	=	dk blue	131	798
–	=	lt brown	369	435
◆	=	med brown	371	434
■	=	dk brown	359	801
•	=	French Knots:		

sleeves—red
border dots—dk blue
eyes—dk brown

| = Backstitch:
mouth, lower border—red
upper border—green
sleeves, lettering—dk blue

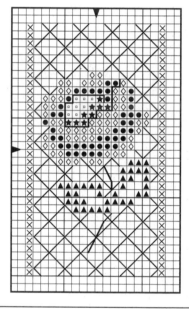

150 Trellis Rose
(18 wide x 32 high)

			Anchor	DMC
◇	=	lt pink	50	605
●	=	dk pink	41	956
▫	=	lt yellow	301	744
★	=	dk yellow	306	783
▲	=	green	257	905
✕	=	blue	343	3752
		= Backstitch:		

flower—dk pink
stem—green
trellis background—blue

151 Country Charmer
(38 wide x 38 high)

			Anchor	DMC
∿	=	white	1	blanc
▫	=	lt pink	25	3326
✪	=	med pink	54	956
●	=	rose	42	326
✳	=	lt peach	336	758
★	=	dk peach	338	922
∿	=	green	227	701
+	=	med blue	977	3755
✕	=	dk blue	979	312
□	=	lt brown	368	437
▣	=	dk brown	370	434
=	=	gray	398	415
■	=	black	403	310
		= Backstitch: black		

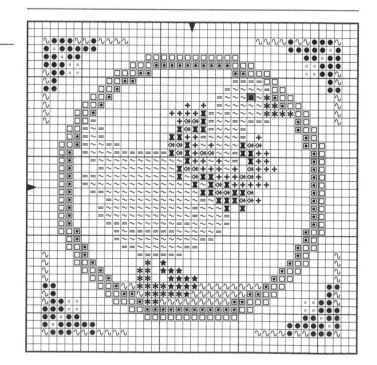

152 Summer Homestead
(57 wide x 63 high)

		Anchor	DMC				Anchor	DMC
▫	= white	1	blanc		⊞ = med blue-gray		850	926
O	= lt rose	969	316		▲ = dk blue-gray		851	3808
●	= dk rose	972	3803		~ = tan		372	738
▣	= fuchsia	89	718		∧ = lt brown		374	420
∿	= yellow	291	444		✕ = med brown		944	434
☆	= lt yellow-green	253	472		✐ = dk brown		360	898
©	= med yellow-green	255	907		☐ = lt taupe		899	3782
★	= dk yellow-green	267	469		⬚ = med taupe		393	640
✕	= very dk yellow-green	269	936		■ = very dk taupe		1041	844
◇	= lt green	1043	369		| = Backstitch:			
#	= med green	243	703		windows—tan			
◆	= dk green	1044	895		stems—very dk taupe			
△	= lt blue-gray	848	927					

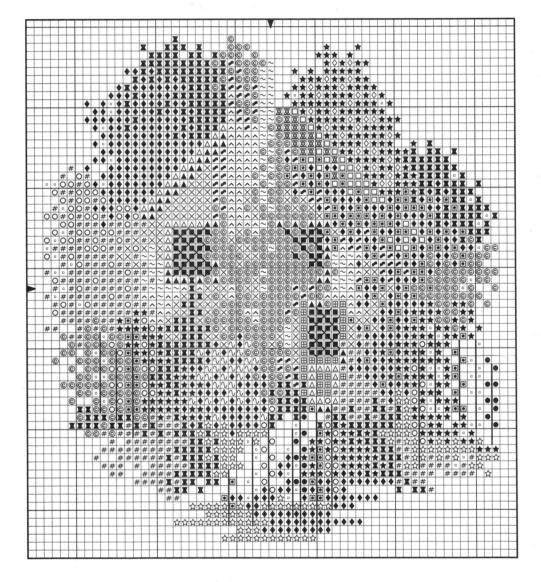

153 Renaissance Rose
(62 wide x 30 high)

		Anchor	DMC				Anchor	DMC
▫	= lt yellow	292	3078	+	= med green		256	704
O	= med yellow	295	726	■	= dk green		258	905
⊙	= med gold	306	725	◆	= rust		349	301
●	= dk gold	307	783	│	= Backstitch: dk gold			
△	= lt green	254	3348					

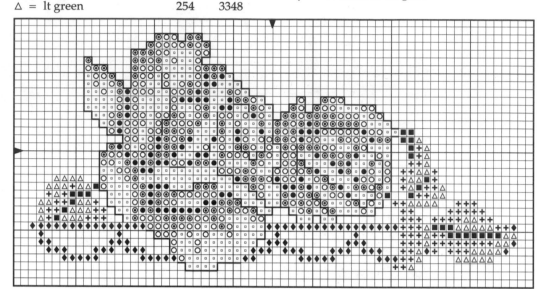

154 Rosebud
(18 wide x 34 high)

		Anchor	DMC
~	= lt rose	25	3326
+	= med rose	40	956
⊙	= med dk rose	42	326
■	= dk rose	1006	304
⊥	= lt yellow-green	256	704
△	= med yellow-green	257	905
#	= med green	258	904
▲	= dk green	246	986
♡	= lt blue	977	334
♥	= dk blue	979	312
│	= Backstitch: med rose		

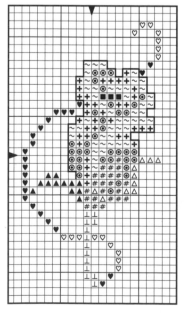

155 Summer Beauty
(43 wide x 45 high)

		Anchor	DMC			Anchor	DMC
~	= very lt rose	48	818	△	= lt green	240	966
+	= lt rose	50	605	#	= med green	209	913
⊙	= med rose	40	335	▲	= dk green	246	986
■	= dk rose	42	326	│	= Backstitch: med rose		

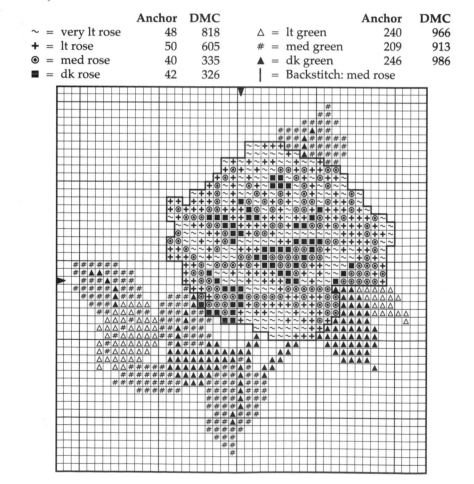

70

156 Cabbage Roses
(68 wide x 32 high)

		Anchor	DMC
▫	= very lt pink	73	963
△	= lt pink	75	962
O	= lt rose	55	957
◉	= med rose	57	602
	dk rose	42	326
+	= orange	328	3341
–	= yellow	301	744
◇	= lt green	265	3348

		Anchor	DMC
#	= med green	266	3347
◆	= dk green	257	905
	very dk green	268	469
	rust	339	920
│	= Backstitch:		
	pink roses—dk rose		
	leaves—very dk green		
	yellow rose—rust		

157 Petite Flower Basket
(26 wide x 27 high)

		Anchor	DMC
♡	= lt pink	50	605
◉	= dk pink	41	956
✕	= red	29	309
▫	= yellow	295	726
✚	= lt green	240	966
▲	= dk green	238	703
∧	= blue	162	517
T	= tan	368	437
■	= brown	370	434

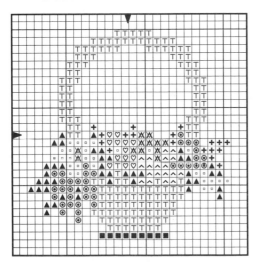

158 Country Goose
(30 wide x 30 high)

		Anchor	DMC
▫	= white	1	blanc
+	= pink	1021	761
✕	= orange	304	741
◇	= yellow	297	973
–	= blue	343	3752
	gray	235	414
●	= black	403	310
│	= Backstitch: gray		

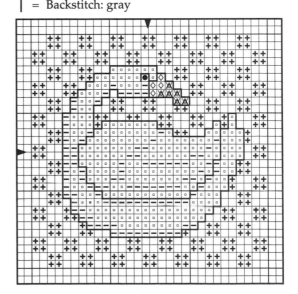

159 Bluebells

(38 wide x 40 high)

			Anchor	DMC
◇	=	lt green	209	913
+	=	med green	227	701
✗	=	dk green	923	3818
○	=	lt blue	130	809
✧	=	med blue	137	798
●	=	dk blue	132	797
│	=	Backstitch: dk green		

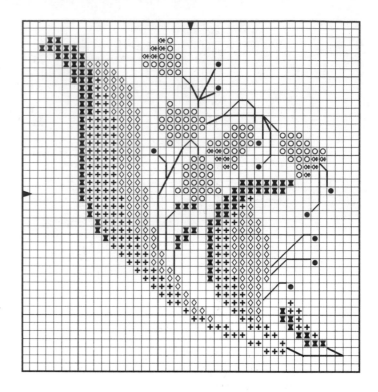

160 Tea Rose

(58 wide x 63 high)

			Anchor	DMC
▫	=	white	1	blanc
~	=	very lt rose	271	819
◇	=	lt rose	24	963
✧	=	med rose	40	956
◉	=	med dk rose	42	326
■	=	dk rose	1006	304
☆	=	lt green	261	989
⋈	=	med green	258	905
▲	=	dk green	245	986

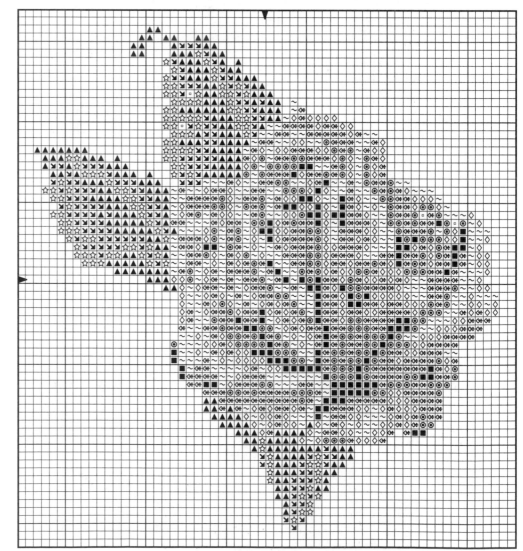

161 Flight Of Fancy

(35 wide x 32 high)

		Anchor	DMC
●	= pink	73	963
~	= lt rose	55	957
✧	= med rose	57	602
◉	= dk rose	42	326
□	= yellow	301	744
△	= lt green	265	3347
▲	= dk green	257	905
+	= brown	370	434
✕	= gray	236	3799
■	= blue-black	127	939

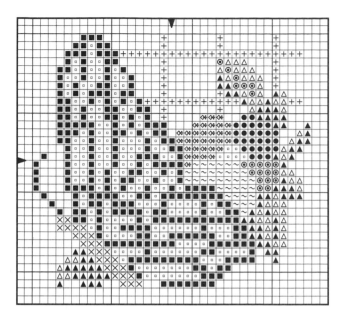

162 Serenity

(40 wide x 69 high)

		Anchor	DMC
▫	= white	1	blanc
○	= lt rose	74	3354
✧	= med rose	76	961
★	= yellow	297	973
✔	= lt yellow-green	265	3347
#	= med yellow-green	266	471
◣	= dk yellow-green	269	936
◇	= green	243	703
✳	= turquoise	187	958
△	= lt blue	1032	3752
⊞	= med blue	1039	518
▲	= blue-gray	850	926
∧	= lt brown	358	433
	med brown	359	801
♥	= dk brown	360	898
■	= black	403	310
•	= French Knots: white		
|	= Backstitch:		
	eye—white		
	stems—dk yellow-green		
	water—turquoise		
	swan—med blue		
	hanging moss—med brown		

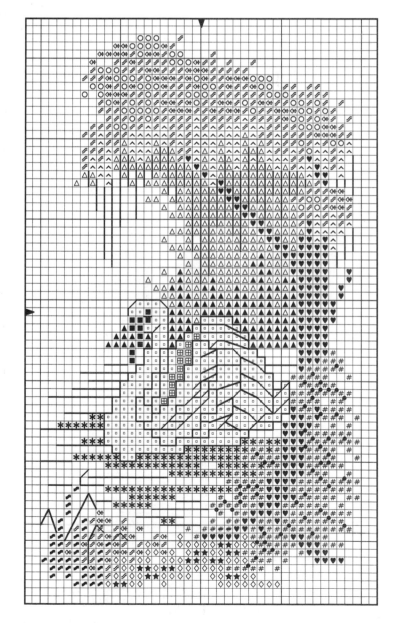

163 Floral Fantasy
(25 wide x 22 high)

		Anchor	DMC
♡	= lt pink	25	3326
#	= med pink	54	956
□	= yellow	295	726
◇	= lt green	238	703
⚊	= med green	245	986
+	= lt blue	130	809
◆	= med blue	132	797
▫	= very lt purple	95	554
○	= lt purple	97	553
◖	= med purple	99	552
●	= dk purple	101	550

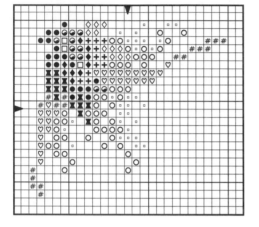

164 Tiny Butterfly
(13 wide x 15 high)

		Anchor	DMC
✖	= blue	131	798
◆	= brown	369	435
■	= gray	236	3799
•	= French Knots: gray		
		= Backstitch: gray		

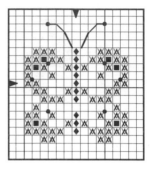

165 Summer Wreath
(30 wide x 30 high)

		Anchor	DMC
▫	= white	1	blanc
▲	= green	238	703
♡	= lt blue	129	809
▦	= med blue	131	798
✳	= dk blue	132	797
~	= purple	111	553

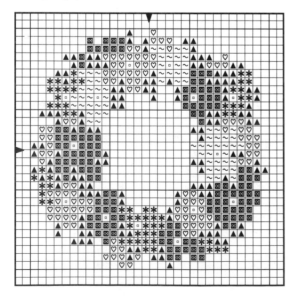

166 Goosedown Comfort
(33 wide x 35 high)

		Anchor	DMC
~	= white	1	blanc
◇	= rose	57	602
✳	= orange	328	3341
+	= blue	137	798
□	= lt purple	96	3609
◣	= med purple	98	553
◉	= dk purple	100	327
#	= lt gray	398	415
■	= dk gray	236	3799
		= Backstitch: lt gray		

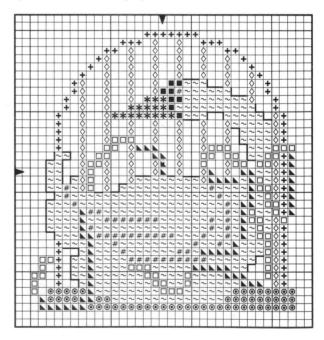

167 **I'll Make A Wish**
(28 wide x 42 high)

		Anchor	DMC
✳	= lt pink	55	957
⊠	= dk pink	63	3804
+	= lt green	238	703
▲	= dk green	245	986
∧	= lt blue-gray	343	3752
◇	= med blue-gray	921	931
~	= tan	367	738
#	= lt brown	369	435
⊙	= med brown	371	434
●	= dk brown	359	801
▫	= gray	398	415

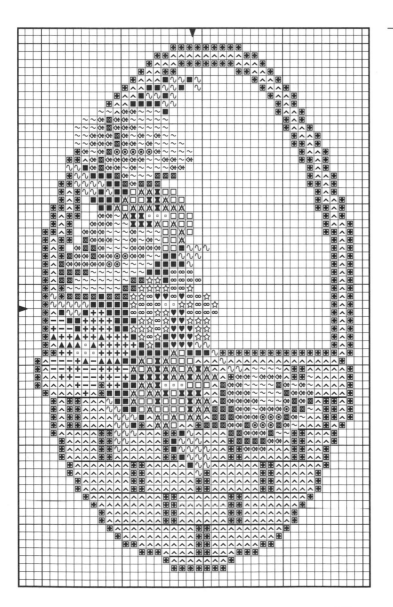

 168 **Flower Basket**
(40 wide x 66 high)

Note: Work half cross stitches for the tan areas of the basket.

		Anchor	DMC
~	= lt pink	55	957
✥	= med pink	54	956
⊠	= red	1006	304
⊙	= fuchsia	62	3806
▫	= yellow	297	973
−	= lt orange	8	3824
+	= med orange	328	3341
▲	= dk orange	330	947
∿	= lt green	238	703
■	= dk green	246	986
□	= lt blue	130	809
✖	= med blue	137	798
✕	= dk blue	132	797
∞	= lt purple	96	3609
☆	= med purple	98	553
♥	= dk purple	100	327
∧	= tan 1/2 cross	368	437
⊞	= brown	358	801
│	= Backstitch: brown		

169 Long-Stemmed Beauty
(61 wide x 111 high)

		Anchor	DMC
O	= med red	46	666
●	= dk red	1006	304
△	= lt green	225	702
+	= med green	227	701
★	= dk green	923	3818

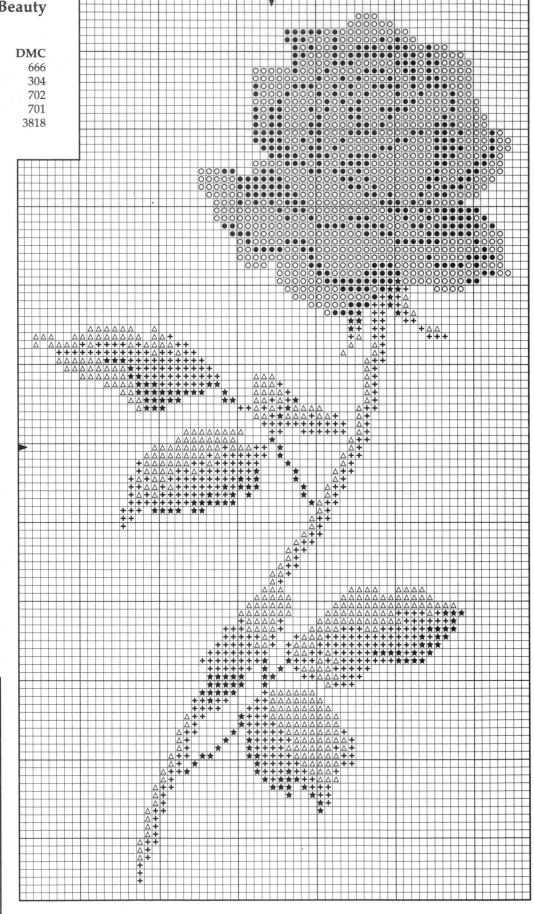

170 Hospitality Pineapple
(19 wide x 29 high)

		Anchor	DMC
O	= gold	306	783
▽	= lt green	265	3347
★	= dk green	238	703
■	= brown	371	434

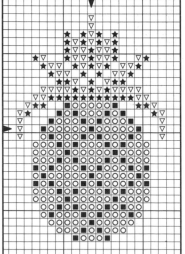

171 Blooms And Butterfly

(26 wide x 27 high)

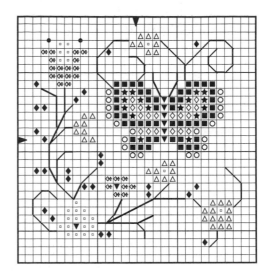

			Anchor	DMC
△	=	lt pink	50	605
★	=	dk pink	40	956
⊶	=	lt orange	328	3341
▼	=	dk orange	330	947
▫	=	yellow	297	973
◆	=	green	257	905
○	=	lt blue	129	809
■	=	dk blue	137	798
◇	=	purple	96	3609
•	=	French Knots: dk pink		
|	=	Backstitch:		
		antennae—dk orange		
		stems—green		

172 Floral Ribbon Heart

(69 wide x 51 high)

			Anchor	DMC				Anchor	DMC
⊶	=	pink	55	957	#	=	med purple	98	553
©	=	orange	328	3341			dk purple	100	327
–	=	yellow	295	726	⋈	=	brown	936	632
◆	=	green	258	987	•	=	French Knots: dk purple		
☆	=	blue	137	798	|	=	Backstitch: dk purple		

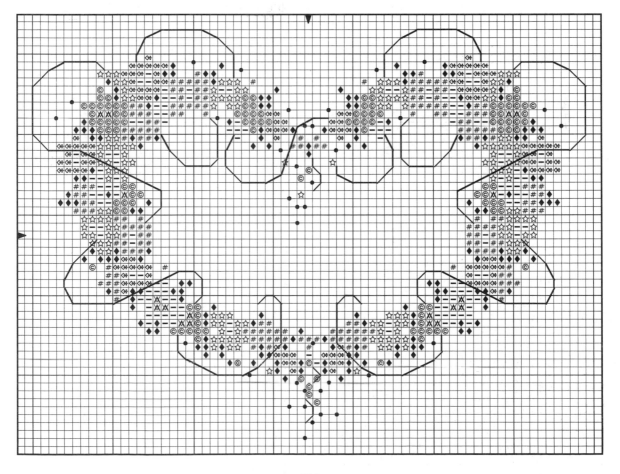

173 Home Is Where...
(23 wide x 29 high)

			Anchor	DMC
✎	=	med rose	1023	3712
★	=	dk rose	896	3721
◇	=	lt green	254	3348
✢	=	med green	238	703
●	=	dk green	245	986
▫	=	blue	130	809
△	=	lt brown	370	434
+	=	dk brown	359	801
◖	=	Lazy Daisies: dk rose		
│	=	Backstitch:		
		stems—dk green		
		lettering—dk brown		

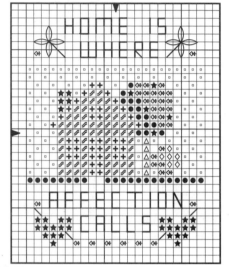

174 Batter Up!
(32 wide x 40 high)

	Anchor	DMC
brown	360	898
│ = Backstitch: brown		

175 Window Garden
(39 wide x 31 high)

			Anchor	DMC
♥	=	rose	57	602
▲	=	green	238	703
□	=	lt blue	130	809
▦	=	dk blue	132	797
⊥	=	brown	349	301

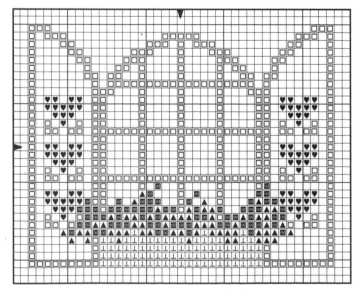

176 Hearts All-Around
(25 wide x 25 high)

			Anchor	DMC
▫	=	lt pink	50	605
◆	=	dk pink	41	956
⋈	=	green	245	986
✢	=	blue	137	798
▼	=	purple	110	208
│	=	Backstitch: green		

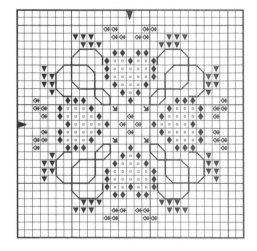

177 Luscious Strawberry
(11 wide x 14 high)

		Anchor	DMC
O =	cream	275	746
● =	red	47	321
△ =	lt green	238	703
	med green	227	701
	=	Backstitch: med green		

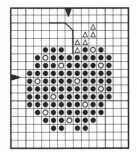

179 Sugar And Spice
(23 wide x 30 high)

		Anchor	DMC
☆ =	pink	55	957
▼ =	red	47	304
□ =	peach	8	3824
△ =	gold	306	783
⋈ =	green	266	3347
	blue	131	798
O =	lt purple	96	3609
★ =	dk purple	100	327
− =	lt brown	369	435
◆ =	med brown	371	434
■ =	dk brown	359	801
• =	French Knots:		
	sleeve—pink		
	border dots—blue		
	=	Backstitch:		
	mouth, lower border—red		
	upper border—green		
	sleeve—dk purple		
	eyes, lettering—dk brown		

178 A Taste Of Country
(25 wide x 24 high)

		Anchor	DMC
△ =	red	29	309
□ =	lt green	240	966
◆ =	dk green	245	986
■ =	black	403	310
• =	French Knot: black		
	=	Backstitch:		
	"Taste"—red		
	"A," "of"—dk green		
	"Country Life"—black		

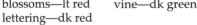

180 Strawberry Blossoms
(25 wide x 25 high)

		Anchor	DMC
□ =	white	1	blanc
◇ =	pink	25	3326
▽ =	lt red	35	3705
◆ =	med red	47	321
♥ =	dk red	44	815
+ =	yellow	297	973
O =	med green	256	704
⋈ =	dk green	258	905
• =	French Knots:		
	"i" dot—dk red		
	strawberry dots—yellow		
	=	Backstitch:		
	blossoms—lt red vine—dk green		
	lettering—dk red		

181 Little Flower Child

(20 wide x 29 high)

		Anchor	DMC
−	= white	1	blanc
◇	= lt pink	50	605
⋈	= dk pink	54	956
○	= peach	8	3824
☆	= med gold	307	783
▽	= dk gold	901	3829
◆	= green	227	701
▫	= lt blue-gray	343	3752
■	= dk blue-gray	921	931
	lt purple	110	208
★	= dk purple	112	552
▲	= brown	370	434

⬭ = Lazy Daisies: dk purple
• = French Knots:
    dress, hat—green
    flowers—lt purple
| = Backstitch: green

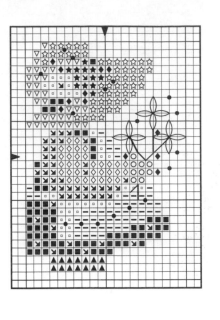

---

182 Floral Wreath

(26 wide x 24 high)

		Anchor	DMC
○	= pink	55	957
+	= rose	63	3804
▫	= yellow	305	743
◆	= green	238	703
◇	= blue	131	798
△	= lt purple	96	3609
●	= brown	371	433

Alphabet

*Use alphabet below to stitch desired initial,
centered in wreath.*

		Anchor	DMC
+	= med purple	98	553

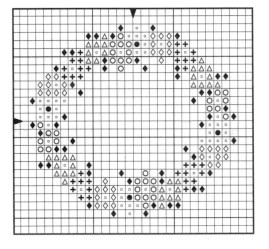

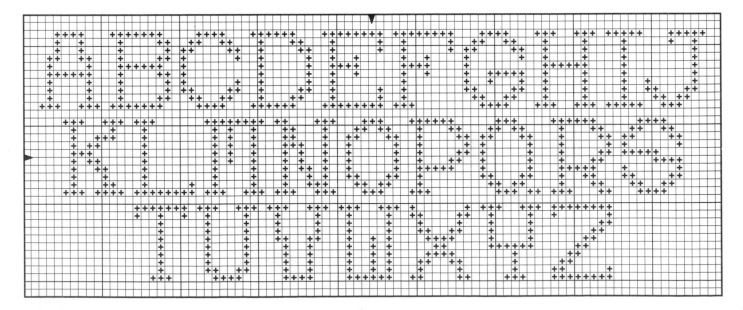

Autumn

Autumn

Autumn

That which you sow — so shall you reap —

Thank you, God for food to eat — milk and bread and honey sweet

Eat apple pie

I LOVE autumn

Come, little leaves, said the wind one day

Autumn Design Directory

The charts are in numerical order beginning on page 86.

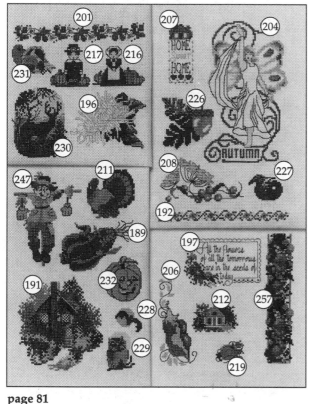

page 81

page 82

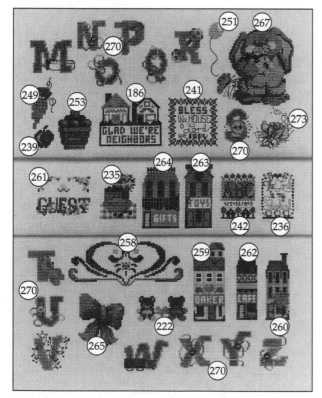

page 83

page 84

183 Wheat Border
(50 wide x 30 high)

		Anchor	DMC
✕ =	brown	371	434
◉ =	rust	1048	3776
❘ =	Backstitch: brown		

184 Large Wheat Motif
(22 wide x 43 high)

		Anchor	DMC
◉ =	rust	1049	3826
❘ =	Backstitch: rust		

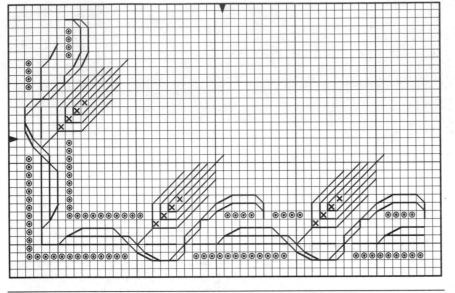

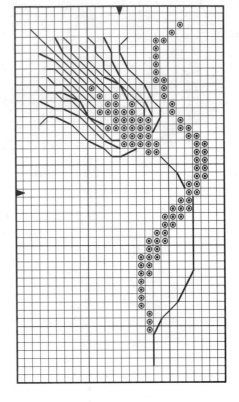

185 Mini Wheat Motif
(32 wide x 14 high)

		Anchor	DMC
✕ =	brown	371	434
❘ =	Backstitch: brown		

186 Glad We're Neighbors
(42 wide x 36 high)

		Anchor	DMC
♥ =	pink	75	962
● =	rose	897	221
☐ =	lt green	876	3816
▲ =	dk green	879	500
◇ =	blue	168	3810
~ =	tan	368	437
O =	lt brown	309	781
■ =	dk brown	358	801

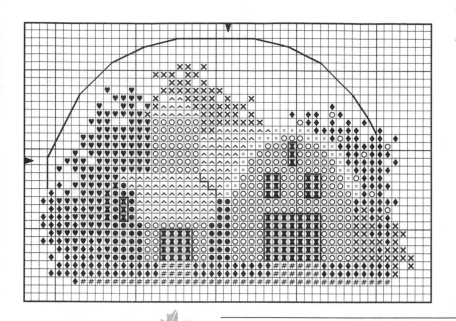

 187 **Country Comfort**
(47 wide x 31 high)

		Anchor	DMC
▫ =	white	1	blanc
○ =	lt red	19	304
● =	dk red	22	814
✕ =	gold	891	676
◆ =	green	266	3347
# =	med rust	347	402
♥ =	dk rust	349	301
^ =	lt gray	398	415
✠ =	dk gray	400	317
| =	Backstitch:		

doors, windows—white
arched border—green
roof—dk gray

188 **Apple Cider**
(34 wide x 28 high)

		Anchor	DMC
▫ =	white	1	blanc
~ =	cream	275	746
✤ =	pink	41	956
○ =	lt red	1024	3328
● =	dk red	19	304
☆ =	yellow	305	743
◇ =	lt green	203	564
▲ =	dk green	211	562
◆ =	yellow-green	924	730
╱ =	lt blue	160	827
◤ =	med blue	977	3755
□ =	lt brown	376	3774
© =	med brown	379	840
■ =	dk brown	936	632
	black	403	310
| =	Backstitch:		

heart, apples—dk red
wallpaper design—dk green

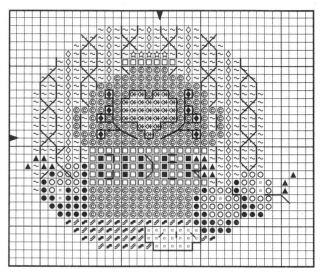

leaf stems on jug—yellow-green
apple stems, lettering—dk brown
seeds—black

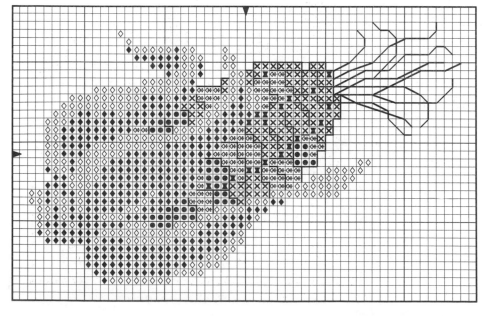

189 **Indian Corn**
(54 wide x 33 high)

		Anchor	DMC
✤ =	med red	1014	355
● =	dk red	20	815
✠ =	very dk red	22	814
✕ =	gold	363	436
◇ =	lt green	261	989
◆ =	dk green	263	3362
| =	Backstitch: very dk red		

190 Thank You, God
(39 wide x 33 high)

	Anchor	DMC
red	22	814

	Kreinik #8 Braid
gold	002HL

- = French Knots:
  lettering—red
  remaining—gold braid
- | = Backstitch:
  lettering—red
  tracery border—gold braid

191 Autumn Homestead
(58 wide x 62 high)

		Anchor	DMC
⟡	= pink	25	3326
●	= red	59	326
✳	= orange	304	741
☆	= yellow	295	726
★	= gold	891	676
♡	= lt yellow-green	265	3347
#	= med yellow-green	267	469
♥	= dk yellow-green	269	936
◆	= green	211	562
⧓	= blue-green	877	3815
U	= lt blue-gray	848	927
+	= med blue-gray	850	926
⊞	= dk blue-gray	851	3808
□	= tan	372	738
⋇	= lt brown	374	420
✒	= dk brown	360	898
^	= lt taupe	899	3782
▼	= med taupe	393	640
■	= dk taupe	906	829
◔	= med rust	369	435
⋈	= dk rust	370	434
	= Backstitch: dk blue-gray		

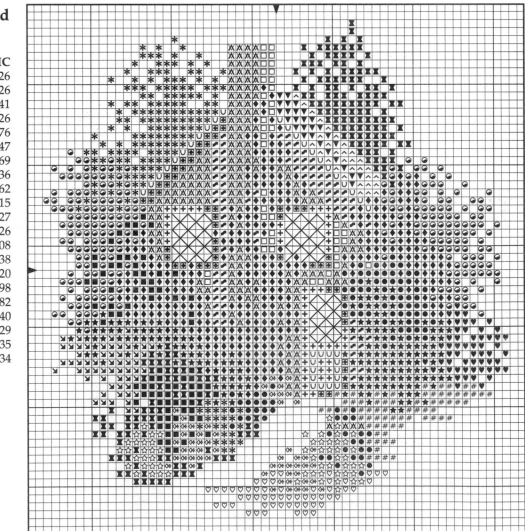

192 Flower Border (24-wide repeat x 7 high)

	Anchor	DMC
● = red	334	606
✿ = orange	304	741
☆ = yellow	288	445
★ = gold	890	729
◆ = green	244	702
□ = lt brown	374	420
■ = dk brown	359	801
│ = Backstitch: green		

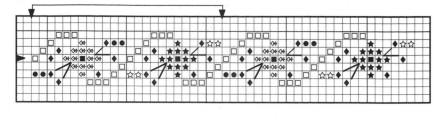

193 Come, Little Leaves (58 wide x 26 high)

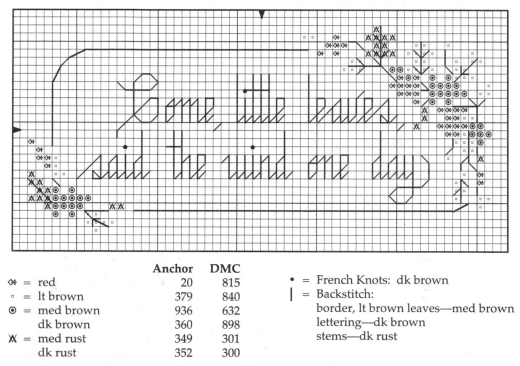

	Anchor	DMC
✿ = red	20	815
▫ = lt brown	379	840
◉ = med brown	936	632
dk brown	360	898
✕ = med rust	349	301
dk rust	352	300

● = French Knots: dk brown
│ = Backstitch:
　border, lt brown leaves—med brown
　lettering—dk brown
　stems—dk rust

194 That Which You Sow (66 wide x 23 high)

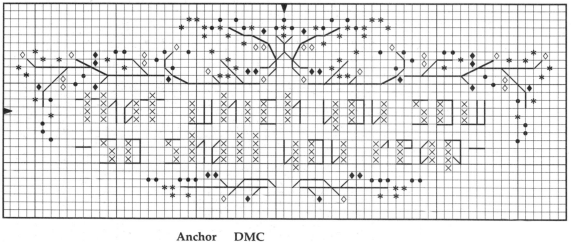

	Anchor	DMC
red	20	815
orange	330	947
◇ = med green	215	320
◆ = dk green	218	319
✕ = rust	1049	3826

● = French Knots: orange
✳ = French Knots: red
│ = Backstitch:
　stems—dk green
　lettering—rust

195   Luscious Pear
(45 wide x 28 high)

		Anchor	DMC
♡	= lt red	893	224
❀	= med red	895	223
♥	= dk red	897	221
~	= lt gold	311	3827
☆	= med gold	901	3829
★	= dk gold	309	781
◇	= lt green	241	966
#	= med green	243	703
◆	= dk green	1044	895
✕	= med brown	359	801
	dk brown	360	898
│	= Backstitch:		
	leaf—dk green		
	tendrils—dk brown		

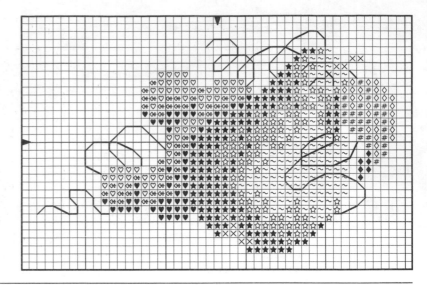

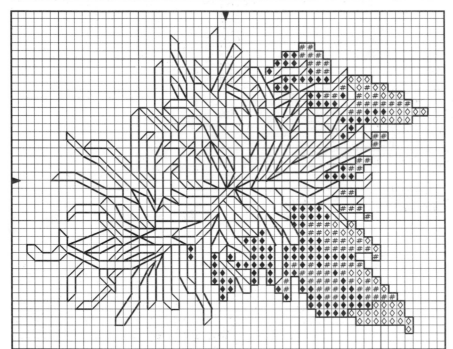

196   Autumn Beauty
(50 wide x 38 high)

		Anchor	DMC
	orange	349	301
◇	= lt green	241	966
#	= med green	244	702
◆	= dk green	1044	895
│	= Backstitch:		
	flower—orange		
	leaves—dk green		

197   All The Flowers
(51 wide x 33 high)

		Anchor	DMC
♡	= med pink	76	961
♥	= dk pink	77	3687
☆	= yellow	305	743
◇	= lt green	264	3348
#	= med green	266	3347
◆	= dk green	262	3363
⊞	= very dk green	269	936
	blue	162	517
✕	= med brown	379	840
	dk brown	360	898
•	= French Knots:		
	lettering—blue		
	remaining—dk brown		
│	= Backstitch:		
	stems—med green		
	lettering—blue		
	remaining—med brown		

198 Flower Basket
(41 wide x 42 high)

		Anchor	DMC
	cream	387	712
☆ =	yellow	295	726
★ =	gold	891	676
♡ =	med rose	1017	316
♥ =	dk rose	1019	3802
▽ =	lt peach	8	3824
◤ =	dk peach	10	351
◇ =	med green	243	703
◆ =	dk green	1044	895
▼ =	purple	109	209
▫ =	lt brown	376	3774
◉ =	med brown	936	632
◢ =	dk brown	360	898
• =	French Knots: purple		
╲ =	Straight Stitch: cream		
│ =	Backstitch: cream		

199 Flower Swag
(39-wide repeat x 15 high)

		Anchor	DMC
▽ =	peach	323	3825
⊕ =	orange	335	606
☆ =	yellow	290	973
◆ =	green	230	699
✕ =	brown	936	632
• =	French Knots: orange		

200 Autumn Leaves
(43 wide x 47 high)

		Anchor	DMC
▫ =	white	1	blanc
☆ =	lt gold	890	729
★ =	dk gold	307	783
▽ =	peach	6	754
⊕ =	orange	324	721
◇ =	lt yellow-green	278	3819
# =	med yellow-green	844	3012
◆ =	dk yellow-green	846	3011
✐ =	med rust	349	301
◤ =	dk rust	352	300
~ =	very lt brown	933	543
+ =	lt brown	378	841
✕ =	med brown	936	632
✗ =	dk brown	360	898
■ =	black	403	310
│ =	Backstitch:		
	eye—black		
	remaining—dk brown		

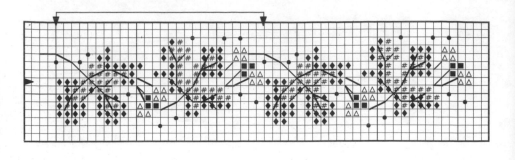

201 Autumn Border

(26-wide repeat x 11 high)

		Anchor	DMC
△	= lt orange	323	3825
■	= dk orange	326	720
#	= green	257	905
◆	= yellow-green	924	730
	brown	371	434
•	= French Knots: dk orange		
|	= Backstitch: brown		

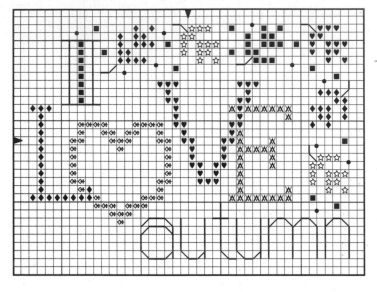

202 I Love Autumn

(40 wide x 29 high)

		Anchor	DMC
✿	= pink	76	961
♥	= red	13	347
☆	= yellow	305	743
◆	= green	246	986
■	= brown	277	420
✕	= rust	1004	920
•	= French Knots: brown		
|	= Backstitch: brown		

203 A Bunch Of Grapes

(55 wide x 50 high)

		Anchor	DMC
◇	= lt green	264	3348
◆	= dk green	268	469
|	= Backstitch: dk green		

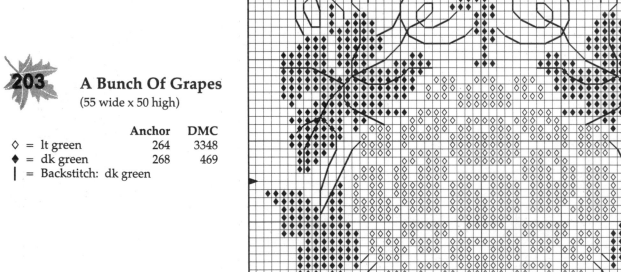

204 **Autumn Fairy** (56 wide x 94 high)

			Anchor	DMC
□	=	white/filament	1/032	blanc/032
−	=	cream/filament	361/032	738/032
~	=	lt peach	1011	948
		med peach	914	407
⋈	=	med orange	5975	356
		dk orange	1015	3777
☆	=	yellow	293	727

Note: For wings, use two strands of floss and one strand of pearl (032) blending filament.

			Anchor	DMC
★	=	gold	306	783
✕	=	yellow-green/filament	261/032	989/032
◇	=	lt blue-green/filament	875/032	3813/032
#	=	med blue-green/filament	877/032	3815/032
		dk blue-green	879	500
		gray	236	3799
•	=	French Knot: med orange		

| = Backstitch:
skin—med peach
dress—dk orange
scarf—dk blue-green
eyes, mouth, skin—gray

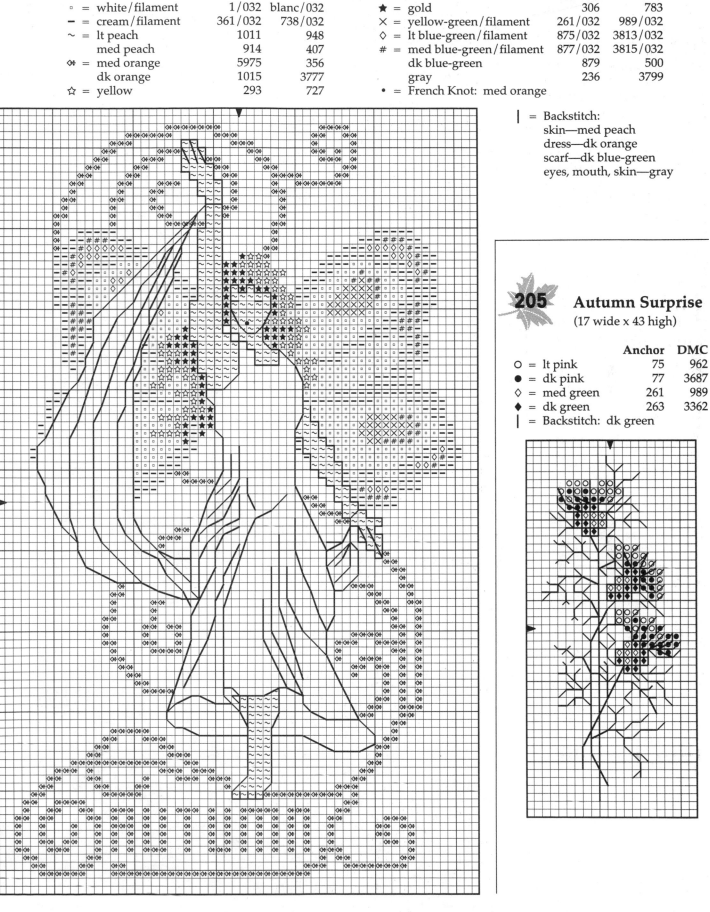

205 **Autumn Surprise**
(17 wide x 43 high)

			Anchor	DMC
○	=	lt pink	75	962
●	=	dk pink	77	3687
◇	=	med green	261	989
◆	=	dk green	263	3362
	=	Backstitch: dk green		

206 Pea Pod Perfection
(26 wide x 60 high)

		Anchor	DMC
~	= very lt yellow-green	259	772
O	= lt yellow-green	253	472
✿	= med yellow-green	255	907
●	= dk yellow-green	258	905
◇	= lt green	213	504
#	= med green	216	502
◆	= dk green	683	890
|	= Backstitch: dk green		

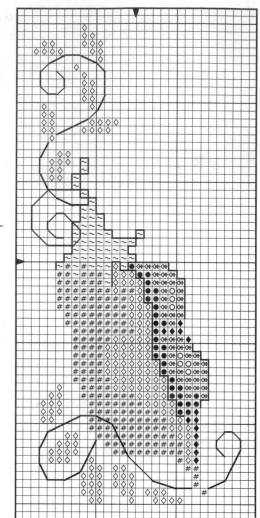

207 Home Sweet Home
(16 wide x 39 high)

		Anchor	DMC
▫	= white	1	blanc
✿	= pink	27	899
●	= red	46	666
#	= med green	216	502
◆	= dk green	218	319
+	= med blue-gray	1034	931
■	= dk blue-gray	1036	3750
◉	= brown	359	801
✎	= rust	1046	435
•	= French Knots: border—pink "Home" (twice)—brown		
|	= Backstitch: border, "Sweet"—pink stems—dk green chimney, remaining lettering—brown		

208 Roadside Blossoms
(57 wide x 30 high)

		Anchor	DMC
▫	= white	1	blanc
~	= cream	933	543
O	= lt blue	939	794
●	= dk blue	940	792
✿	= med brown	378	841
■	= dk brown	359	801
|	= Backstitch: flowers—med brown leaf stems—dk brown		

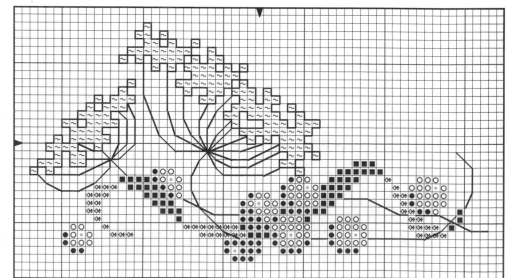

209 Country Quail
(32 wide x 35 high)

		Anchor	DMC
▫	= white	1	blanc
✕	= blue	122	3807
ω	= brown	393	640
○	= lt rust	1047	402
✿	= med rust	1048	3776
➤	= dk rust	1049	3826
~	= lt gray	234	762
⊙	= med gray	399	318
⊠	= dk gray	400	317
■	= black	403	310
		= Backstitch:	
	under eye—white		
	remaining—dk gray		

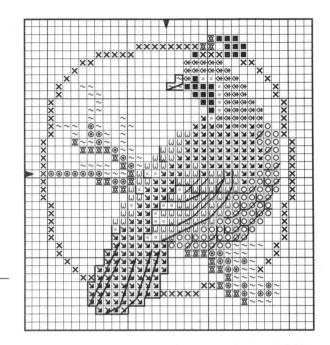

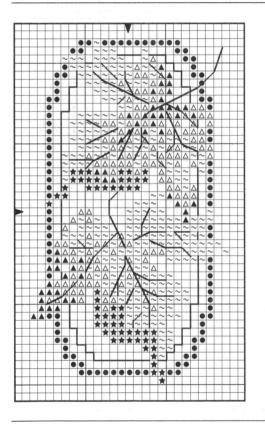

210 Colors Of Fall
(25 wide x 43 high)

		Anchor	DMC
~	= cream	942	738
△	= lt orange	323	3825
▲	= dk orange	329	3340
★	= gold	363	436
	med brown	357	433
●	= dk brown	359	801
		= Backstitch:	
	leaf veins, stems—med brown		
	border—dk brown		

211 Tom Turkey
(32 wide x 31 high)

		Anchor	DMC
▫	= white	1	blanc
●	= red	1025	347
▲	= orange	316	970
✿	= blue	137	798
➤	= brown	359	801
○	= lt rust	347	402
⌇	= med rust	369	435
➘	= dk rust	370	434
■	= black	403	310
		= Backstitch:	
	eye—black		
	remaining—brown		

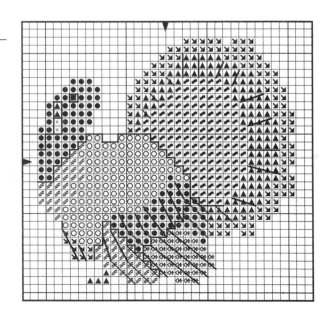

212 Little Cottage
(31 wide x 20 high)

		Anchor	DMC
▫	= white	1	blanc
✿	= pink	1013	3778
☆	= yellow	874	834
◇	= lt green	243	703
◆	= dk green	1044	895
○	= lt blue-gray	848	927
●	= dk blue-gray	850	926
#	= brown	358	801
◉	= rust	352	300
∧	= gray	398	415
■	= black	403	310
		= Backstitch:		
	house—dk blue-gray		
	trees—rust		

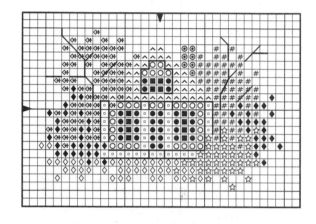

213 Baby Bird
(28 wide x 26 high)

		Anchor	DMC
~	= very lt peach	1009	3770
○	= lt peach	1012	754
✿	= med peach	882	758
◉	= med dk peach	1008	3773
◢	= dk peach	1007	3772
✳	= orange	10	351
★	= gold	891	676
◇	= lt yellow-green	279	734
#	= med yellow-green	843	3012
◆	= dk yellow-green	846	3011
✕	= blue	158	747
	brown	360	898
■	= black	403	310
•	= French Knots: orange		
		= Backstitch:		
	bird outline & neck, leaf veins—dk peach		
	feathers, stems—brown		
	eye—black		

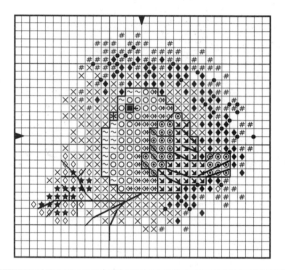

214 Green Pepper
(28 wide x 25 high)

		Anchor	DMC
~	= yellow-green	843	3012
◇	= lt green	205	912
#	= med green	245	986
◆	= dk green	1044	895
		= Backstitch: dk green		

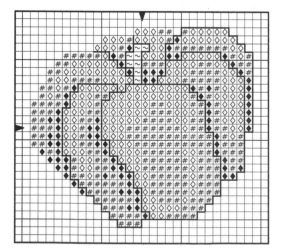

215 Helmet
(21 wide x 20 high)

		Anchor	DMC
☆	= yellow	298	972
●	= blue	139	797
		= Backstitch: blue		

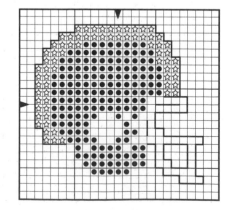

216 Pilgrim Woman
(34 wide x 26 high)

		Anchor	DMC
▫	= white	1	blanc
⊙	= pink	23	3713
~	= peach	1010	951
△	= med orange	323	3825
▲	= dk orange	316	970
#	= green	244	702
❖	= med brown	310	780
●	= dk brown	351	400
■	= black	403	310
•	= French Knot: black		
│	= Backstitch:		

face (except eyes), hands, pumpkins—med brown
hair, eyes, apron sides—black

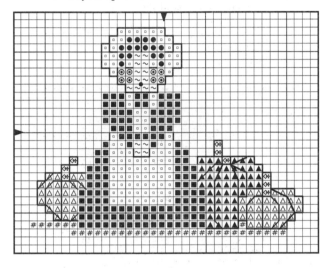

217 Pilgrim Man
(26 wide x 28 high)

		Anchor	DMC
▫	= white	1	blanc
⊙	= pink	23	3713
~	= peach	1010	951
△	= med orange	323	3825
▲	= dk orange	316	970
☆	= yellow	306	783
#	= green	244	702
❖	= med brown	310	780
●	= dk brown	359	801
■	= black	403	310
•	= French Knots:		

buttons—yellow
mouth—black

│ = Backstitch:
inner lines of clothes—white
face (except eyes), hands, pumpkins—med brown
eyes, cuffs, collar, shoes, hat—black

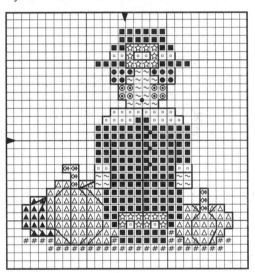

218 Hot Apple Pie
(24 wide x 17 high)

		Anchor	DMC
	red	1025	347
∧	= blue-gray	274	927
▫	= lt brown	276	739
❖	= med brown	369	435
■	= dk brown	371	434
•	= French Knots: dk brown		
│	= Backstitch:		

lettering—red
lower edge of crust—med brown
remaining—dk brown

219 Pumpkin
(19 wide x 15 high)

		Anchor	DMC
△	= med orange	324	721
	dk orange	333	608
#	= med green	266	3347
♦	= dk green	269	936
■	= brown	358	801
│	= Backstitch:		

pumpkin—dk orange
tendrils—dk green

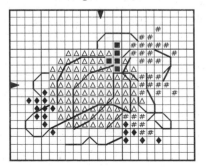

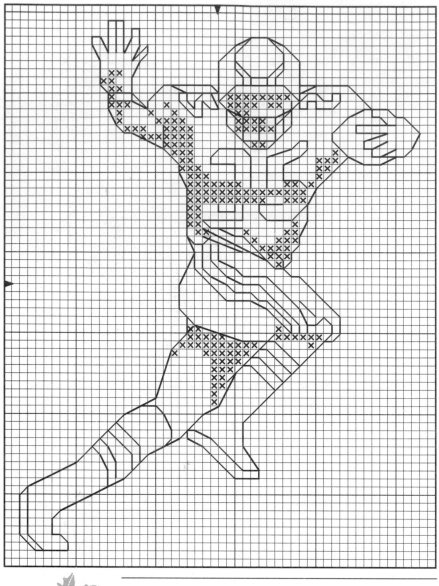

220 Football Time
(50 wide x 66 high)

		Anchor	DMC
✕ =	brown	1041	844
	=	Backstitch: brown		

221 Bouquet
(27 wide x 47 high)

		Anchor	DMC
~ =	very lt pink	49	963
○ =	lt pink	50	605
◗ =	med pink	68	3687
● =	dk pink	65	3685
∧ =	lt yellow	301	744
◇ =	med yellow	305	743
☆ =	gold	307	783
▽ =	very lt green	259	772
◣ =	lt green	265	3348
★ =	med green	216	502
■ =	dk green	217	561
− =	lt blue	159	3325
✪ =	med blue	161	813
✳ =	rust	351	400
	=	Backstitch: dk green		

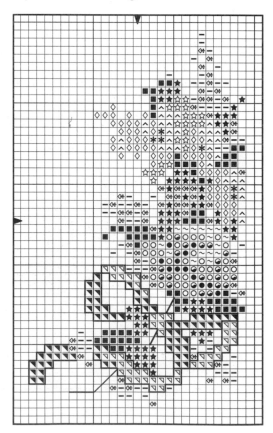

222 Pair of Bears
(35 wide x 17 high)

		Anchor	DMC
✪ =	pink	40	956
~ =	tan	4146	950
✕ =	lt brown	914	3773
⊙ =	med brown	936	632
▲ =	dk brown	360	898
✎ =	gray-black	236	3799
• =	French Knots:		
	left bear—tan	right bear—lt brown	

98

223 Mushroom
(21 wide x 24 high)

		Anchor	DMC
~	= cream	361	738
✿	= rust	1048	3776
☐	= lt brown	358	801
■	= dk brown	360	898
|	= Backstitch: dk brown		

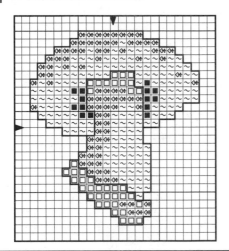

224 Shades Of Autumn
(23 wide x 21 high)

		Anchor	DMC
O	= yellow	295	726
☆	= lt gold	891	676
#	= med gold	307	783
★	= dk gold	309	781
⊻	= brown	358	801
|	= Backstitch: brown		

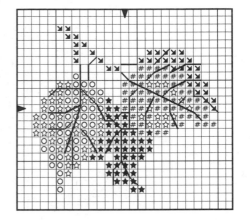

225 Autumn Berries
(29 wide x 30 high)

		Anchor	DMC
◇	= lt green	209	913
◆	= dk green	212	561
~	= lt yellow-green	842	3013
⊙	= med yellow-green	843	3012
⊻	= dk yellow-green	845	730
O	= lt blue	144	800
✿	= med blue	147	797
●	= dk blue	150	823
|	= Backstitch:		
	stems—dk yellow-green		
	berries—med blue		

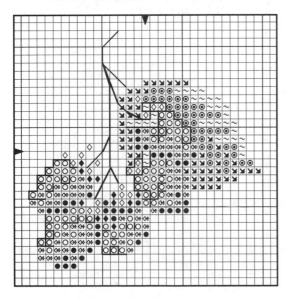

226 The Acorn
(35 wide x 34 high)

		Anchor	DMC
▫	= white	1	blanc
◇	= med green	261	989
◆	= dk green	263	3362
●	= brown	906	829
⌃	= lt rust	368	437
⊙	= med rust	369	435
⊻	= dk rust	352	300
	black	403	310
|	= Backstitch: black		

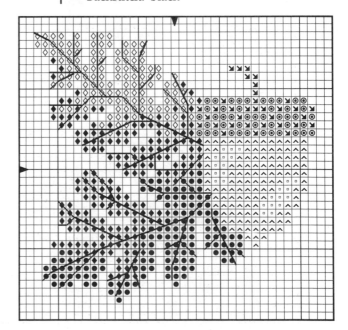

227 Crisp Apple
(23 wide x 17 high)

			Anchor	DMC
□	=	white	1	blanc
✥	=	med red	47	321
●	=	dk red	20	815
▼	=	orange	316	970
☆	=	yellow	288	445
◇	=	lt green	242	989
◆	=	dk green	246	986
■	=	brown	359	801
│	=	Backstitch: brown		

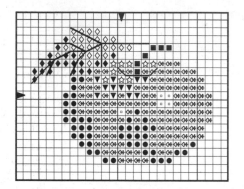

228 Bat In The Night
(18 wide x 16 high)

			Anchor	DMC
☆	=	yellow	298	972
■	=	black	403	310

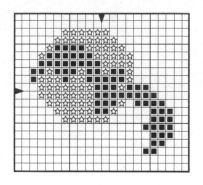

229 Wise Old Owl
(19 wide x 26 high)

			Anchor	DMC
★	=	gold	301	744
△	=	lt brown	376	3774
#	=	med brown	379	840
▲	=	dk brown	359	801
○	=	lt rust	943	422
◉	=	med rust	944	434
⋈	=	dk rust	310	780
■	=	black	403	310
│	=	Backstitch:		
		feathers—dk brown		
		face—dk rust		
		beak—black		

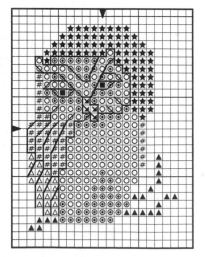

230 The Mighty Stag
(40 wide x 46 high)

			Anchor	DMC
△	=	orange	314	741
✕	=	yellow	293	727
#	=	med red-orange	11	351
◆	=	dk red-orange	13	347
●	=	brown	358	801
│	=	Backstitch: brown		

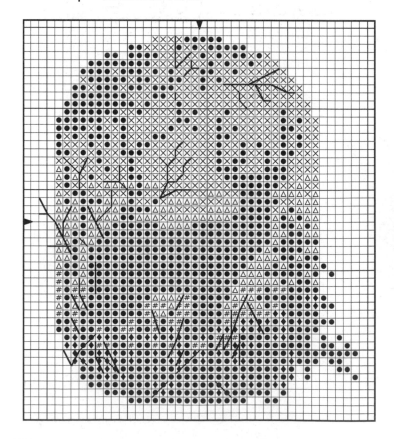

231 Horn Of Plenty
(29 wide x 20 high)

		Anchor	DMC
●	= red	47	321
▲	= orange	316	970
☆	= yellow	290	973
#	= yellow-green	254	3348
◇	= lt green	206	564
◆	= dk green	217	561
♥	= purple	101	550
□	= lt brown	376	3774
◉	= med brown	378	841
■	= dk brown	936	632
		= Backstitch: dk brown		

232 Jack O' Lantern
(25 wide x 29 high)

		Anchor	DMC
☆	= yellow	305	743
△	= lt orange	323	3825
▲	= dk orange	329	3340
◇	= med green	260	772
◆	= dk green	262	3363
#	= med brown	359	801
■	= dk brown	380	838
		= Backstitch:		
	leaf—dk green		
	pumpkin—med brown		face, stem—dk brown

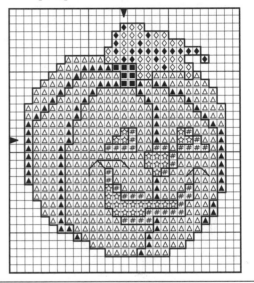

233 Country Hideaway (59 wide x 34 high)

		Anchor	DMC			Anchor	DMC
▫	= white	1	blanc	☆ = gold	891	676
○	= lt red	1022	760	ℐ = yellow-green	266	3347
✤	= med red	1025	347	# = med green	210	562
●	= dk red	1015	3777	◆ = dk green	879	500
△	= med orange	313	742	✕ = brown	889	610
▲	= dk orange	316	970	◉ = gray	235	414
					= Backstitch: gray		

234 Peach Jelly
(22 wide x 22 high)

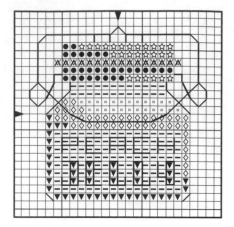

		Anchor	DMC
−	= white	2	blanc
◊	= lt peach	328	3341
▼	= dk peach	11	351
▫	= lt yellow	300	745
☆	= lt green	215	320
●	= dk green	217	561
	blue-gray	921	931
⋈	= rust	355	975
	dk brown	357	433
|	= Backstitch:		
	"Jelly"—dk peach		
	handle—dk green		
	"Peach"—blue-gray		
	jar—dk brown		

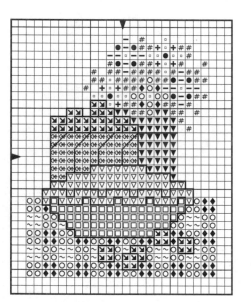

235 Kitchen Cookin'
(24 wide x 30 high)

		Anchor	DMC
~	= white	2	blanc
−	= lt pink	24	776
●	= dk pink	27	899
⋈	= red	44	815
▫	= lt yellow	293	727
+	= dk yellow	307	783
#	= green	267	469
O	= lt blue	159	3325
◆	= dk blue	161	826
▽	= lt brown	362	437
⊕	= med brown	373	3828
▼	= dk brown	371	434
	very dk brown	357	433
□	= gray	399	318
|	= Backstitch: very dk brown		

236 The Lord Is My Shepherd
(21 wide x 31 high)

		Anchor	DMC
▫	= white	2	blanc
	pink	76	961
★	= red	20	498
◊	= lt green	266	3347
▼	= dk green	246	986
■	= black	403	310
•	= French Knots:		
	border dots—red		
	"i" dot—dk green		
|	= Backstitch:		
	"Lord," "Shepherd"—pink		
	stems—lt green		
	"The," "is my"—dk green		
	sheep—black		

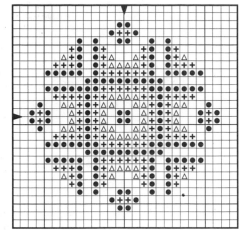

237 Country Star
(24 wide x 24 high)

		Anchor	DMC
△	= lt purple	109	209
+	= dk purple	101	550
●	= black	403	310

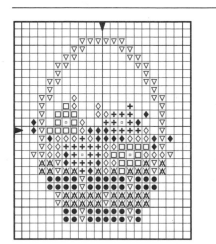

238 Basket Of Posies
(18 wide x 23 high)

		Anchor	DMC
□	= lt pink	74	3354
+	= dk pink	42	326
▫	= yellow	293	727
◇	= lt green	266	3347
◆	= dk green	268	469
▽	= lt brown	363	436
✕	= med brown	371	433
●	= dk brown	360	898

239 Mini Apple
(13 wide x 15 high)

		Anchor	DMC
✢	= pink	26	894
●	= red	47	321
⌄	= brown	357	433

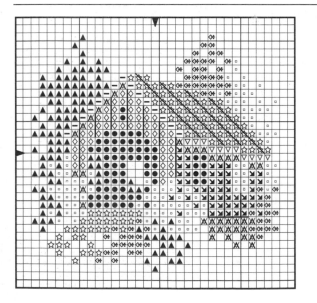

240 Covered Bridge
(31 wide x 30 high)

		Anchor	DMC
–	= white	2	blanc
▫	= lt green	266	471
✢	= med green	257	905
▲	= dk green	246	986
☆	= lt brown	373	3828
✕	= med brown	357	433
●	= dk brown	381	938
◇	= lt rust	5975	356
⌄	= dk rust	1015	3777
▽	= gray	399	318
|	= Backstitch: dk brown		

241 Bless This House

(33 wide x 33 high)

		Anchor	DMC
♥ =	red	69	3687
▫ =	gold	887	3046
◆ =	green	267	469
+ =	blue-gray	921	931
☆ =	purple	100	327
	brown	357	433

• = French Knot: green

| = Backstitch:
   "O," "Pray"—red
   "this"—green
   "Lord"—blue-gray
   "House," "We"—brown

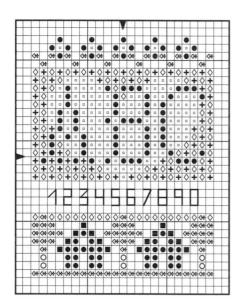

242 ABC Sampler

(23 wide x 30 high)

		Anchor	DMC
▫ =	pink	76	961
● =	red	44	815
✹ =	green	266	3347
◇ =	lt blue	128	800
+ =	med blue	121	809
○ =	lt brown	309	781
■ =	dk brown	381	938
| =	Backstitch: red		

243 Floral Kaleidoscope

(31 wide x 31 high)

		Anchor	DMC
▫ =	lt pink	24	776
◆ =	dk pink	11	351
♥ =	red	897	221
◇ =	lt green	242	989
★ =	dk green	245	986
+ =	blue-gray	922	930
▽ =	purple	96	3609

• = French Knots: purple

| = Backstitch:
   leaf stems—lt green
   flower stems—dk green

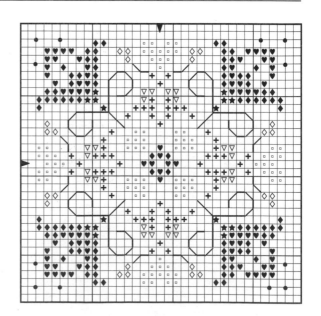

104

244 Country Cottage
(23 wide x 31 high)

		Anchor	DMC
—	= white	2	blanc
	pink	74	3354
+	= red	1015	3777
◇	= lt green	266	3347
◆	= dk green	268	469
▫	= tan	942	738
☆	= lt brown	369	435
⋈	= med brown	352	300
▼	= dk brown	381	938

• = French Knots:
  roof decoration, shutters—pink
  flowers—red

| = Backstitch:
  window panes—white
  cottage, chimney top, door, shutters
    —med brown
  chimney bricks—dk brown

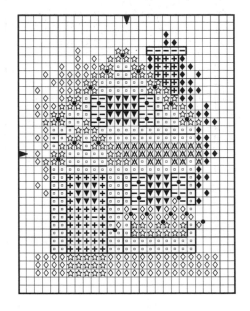

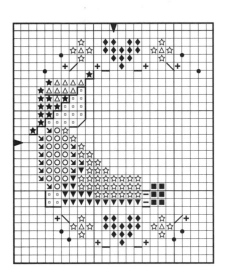

245 Country Boy
(21 wide x 26 high)

		Anchor	DMC
—	= white	2	blanc
○	= med pink	27	899
⋈	= dk pink	69	3687
◆	= red	59	326
▫	= lt peach	778	754
	med peach	914	407
△	= lt yellow	295	726
★	= dk yellow	890	729
+	= green	256	906
☆	= lt blue	167	519
▼	= med blue	168	3810
■	= brown	371	433

• = French Knots: dk pink

| = Backstitch:
  face, hand—med peach
  stems—green
  hat brim, sock—brown

246 Country Girl
(18 wide x 26 high)

		Anchor	DMC
—	= white	2	blanc
○	= med pink	27	899
⋈	= dk pink	69	3687
◆	= red	59	326
▫	= peach	778	754
+	= green	256	906
☆	= lt blue	167	519
▼	= med blue	168	3810
■	= brown	371	433

• = French Knots: dk pink

| = Backstitch:
  face, hand—med pink
  sock, apron—dk pink
  stems—green

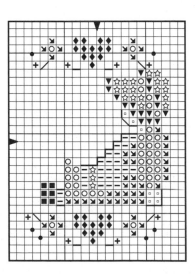

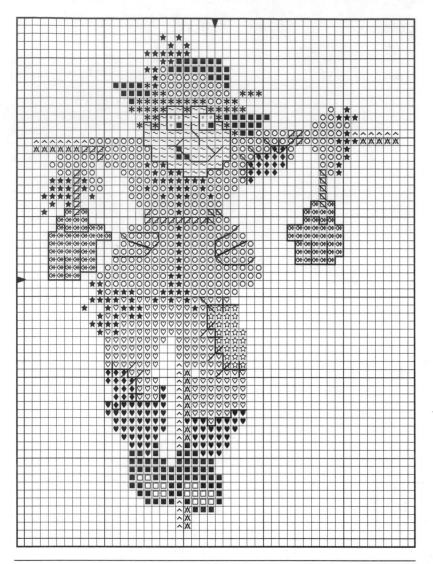

247 Silly Scarecrow
(46 wide x 62 high)

			Anchor	DMC
▫	=	white	1	blanc
✿	=	pink	31	3708
~	=	peach	6	754
✳	=	orange	326	720
☆	=	yellow	298	972
★	=	gold	307	783
◆	=	green	210	562
○	=	lt blue	129	809
		dk blue	132	797
□	=	lt brown	375	869
■	=	dk brown	359	801
♡	=	lt rust	1048	3776
♥	=	dk rust	1004	920
^	=	lt gray	398	415
✕	=	med gray	235	414
		dk gray	236	3799
		=	Backstitch:		

pocket stitching—dk blue
face—dk brown
arms, gloves, remaining patchwork
  stitching—dk gray

248 Cheerful Heart
(21 wide x 24 high)

			Anchor	DMC
✎	=	lt pink	24	963
✿	=	med pink	27	899
♥	=	dk pink	59	498
□	=	yellow	295	726
+	=	green	243	703

249 Grape Cluster
(16 wide x 35 high)

			Anchor	DMC
○	=	lt green	208	563
#	=	med green	856	370
◆	=	dk green	862	520
		=	Backstitch:		

grapes—med green
tendrils, leaf—dk green

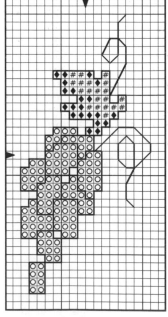

250 Bountiful Fruit
(24 wide x 24 high)

		Anchor	DMC
●	= red	19	304
✦	= orange	329	3340
▫	= yellow	291	444
△	= gold	307	783
☆	= green	256	704
✚	= blue	168	3810
▼	= purple	98	553
○	= tan	362	437
	brown	360	898
	= Backstitch: brown		

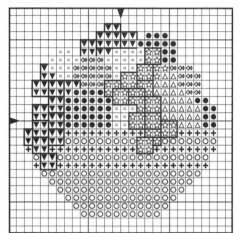

251 Balloon
(10 wide x 36 high)

		Anchor	DMC
ʌ	= white	2	blanc
○	= blue	167	519
	gray	236	3799
	= Backstitch: gray		

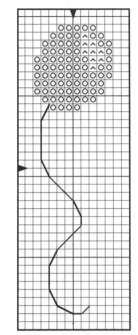

252 Favorite Teddy
(57 wide x 55 high)

		Anchor	DMC
▫	= white	2	blanc
✦	= lt rose	25	3716
➤	= dk rose	77	3687
◇	= lt yellow	295	726
♥	= dk yellow	307	783
△	= lt green	214	368
#	= med green	205	912
▲	= dk green	923	699
◉	= med blue	433	996
●	= dk blue	410	995
~	= tan	387	712
=	= lt brown	362	437
✚	= med brown	309	781
⋈	= dk brown	357	433
■	= very dk brown	382	3371
	= Backstitch:		
	teddy (except eyelashes),		
	ribbon, flowers—dk brown		
	eyelashes— very dk brown		

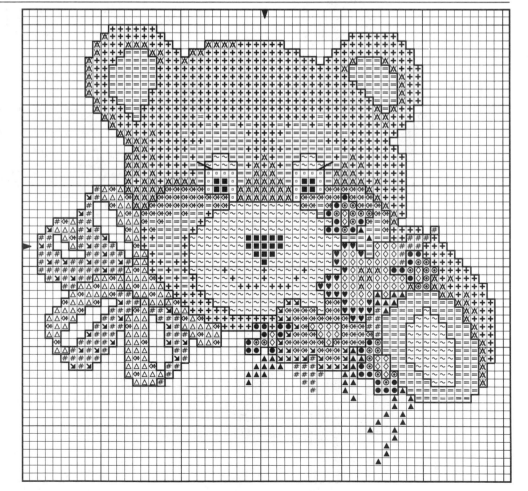

253 Basket Of Apples
(22 wide x 27 high)

			Anchor	DMC
−	=	pink	26	894
◇	=	lt red	35	3801
◆	=	med red	47	321
★	=	dk red	20	498
●	=	very dk red	72	902
▫	=	lt brown	373	422
○	=	med brown	309	781
▼	=	dk brown	357	433
		=	Backstitch:		

apples—very dk red
remaining—dk brown

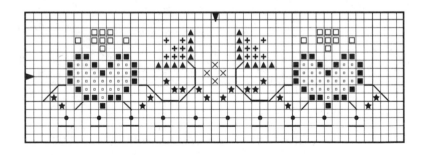

254 Share A Little Love
(18 wide x 24 high)

			Anchor	DMC
		red	35	3801
○	=	yellow	297	973
◆	=	green	257	905
★	=	brown	371	433
•	=	French Knots:		

flowers—red
lettering—brown

| | | = | Backstitch: | | |

stems—green
lettering—brown

255 Hearts And Flowers
(43 wide x 12 high)

			Anchor	DMC
▫	=	pink	25	3326
■	=	red	59	326
□	=	yellow	290	973
★	=	green	256	906
+	=	med blue	137	798
▲	=	dk blue	133	796
×	=	purple	98	553
•	=	French Knots: green		
		=	Backstitch: green		

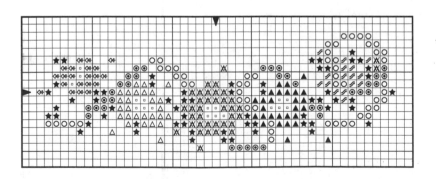

256 Garland
(45 wide x 15 high)

			Anchor	DMC
◆	=	pink	28	3706
⁄	=	orange	329	3340
▫	=	yellow	301	744
○	=	lt gold	363	436
⊙	=	dk gold	369	435
★	=	green	239	702
△	=	lt blue	160	813
▲	=	dk blue	162	825
✕	=	purple	98	553

257 Harvest Border

(20 wide x 43-high repeat)

		Anchor	DMC
♡	= lt rose	893	224
+	= med rose	895	223
♥	= dk rose	897	221
◉	= med peach	9	352
●	= dk peach	11	351
☆	= med gold	363	436
★	= dk gold	365	435
~	= very lt yellow-green	259	772
◇	= lt yellow-green	265	3347
#	= med yellow-green	268	469
♦	= dk yellow-green	862	520
□	= lt blue	145	809
◈	= med blue	146	798
■	= dk blue	148	312
⁄	= med purple	109	209
↝	= dk purple	102	550
│	= Backstitch:		

rose berries—dk rose
lt yellow-green leaves, pear
    stems—dk yellow-green
blue berries—dk blue

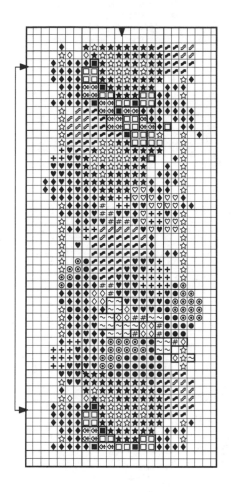

258 Folk Art

(77 wide x 30 high)

		Anchor	DMC			Anchor	DMC
●	= red	42	326	✳	= med blue	121	809
○	= yellow	297	444	■	= dk blue	122	792
▲	= green	879	500	◌	= Lazy Daisies: dk blue		

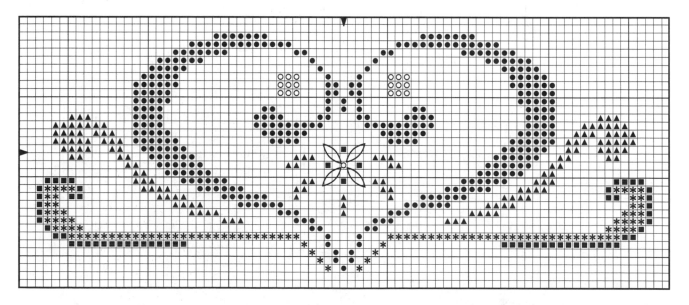

259 The Baker
(21 wide x 53 high)

			Anchor	DMC
▫	=	white	2	blanc
⊞	=	rose	894	223
◇	=	lt green	261	989
●	=	dk green	258	987
×	=	turquoise	158	747
■	=	gray	236	3799
•	=	French Knots: gray		

260 Bed & Breakfast
(16 wide x 45 high)

			Anchor	DMC
~	=	cream	366	951
○	=	rose	65	3685
◇	=	lt green	261	989
●	=	dk green	258	987
□	=	blue	849	932
✎	=	rust	351	400
+	=	brown	379	840
■	=	gray	236	3799
•	=	French Knots: gray		

261 Guest
(36 wide x 26 high)

			Anchor	DMC
♡	=	pink	24	963
✧	=	orange	313	742
+	=	lt green	261	989
▲	=	dk green	263	3362
○	=	blue	9159	828
ω	=	purple	103	211
■	=	rust	308	781

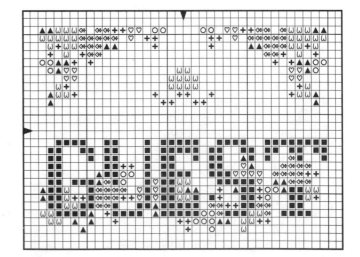

262 Cafe
(14 wide x 46 high)

		Anchor	DMC
□ =	white	2	blanc
~ =	cream	366	951
● =	green	258	987
☐ =	lt blue	849	932
★ =	dk blue	851	924
✎ =	rust	351	400
+ =	med brown	379	840
♥ =	dk brown	360	898
■ =	gray	236	3799
• =	French Knot: gray		

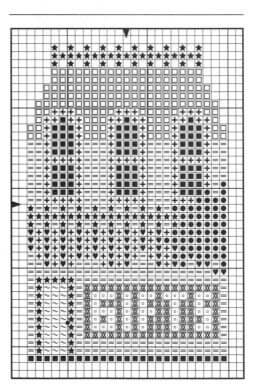

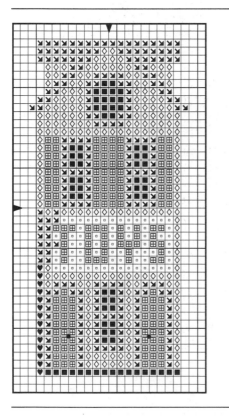

263 Toy Shop
(20 wide x 42 high)

		Anchor	DMC
□ =	white	2	blanc
⊞ =	rose	894	223
◇ =	lt green	261	989
✄ =	dk green	258	987
♥ =	brown	360	898
■ =	gray	236	3799
• =	French Knots: gray		

264 Gift Shop
(25 wide x 40 high)

		Anchor	DMC
□ =	white	2	blanc
~ =	cream	366	951
= =	peach	9575	3830
● =	green	258	905
☐ =	lt blue	849	932
★ =	dk blue	851	924
⊠ =	rust	347	402
+ =	med brown	379	840
♥ =	dk brown	360	898
■ =	gray	236	3799
• =	French Knot: gray		

265 Green Bow

(31 wide x 38 high)

		Anchor	DMC
~	= lt green	875	3813
⚹	= med green	877	3815
■	= dk green	879	500

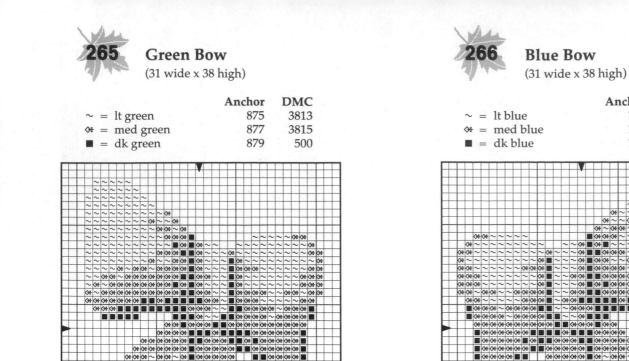

266 Blue Bow

(31 wide x 38 high)

		Anchor	DMC
~	= lt blue	120	3747
⚹	= med blue	122	3807
■	= dk blue	123	820

267 Bunny

(52 wide x 53 high)

		Anchor	DMC
⚹	= pink	892	225
⊕	= med red	42	326
	dk red	47	321
✎	= orange	304	741
☆	= med yellow	305	743
★	= dk yellow	306	725
✖	= green	879	500
△	= lt blue	160	827
#	= med blue	162	825
▲	= dk blue	164	824
○	= tan	942	738
◕	= rust	324	922
◇	= lt brown	363	436
+	= med brown	310	434
◆	= dk brown	357	433
■	= very dk brown	382	3371
•	= French Knots:		
	flower buds—dk red		
	antennae—dk brown		
│	= Backstitch:		
	flower—dk yellow		
	stems, grass—green		
	muzzle—dk brown		
	antennae, eyes, eyebrows—very		
	dk brown		

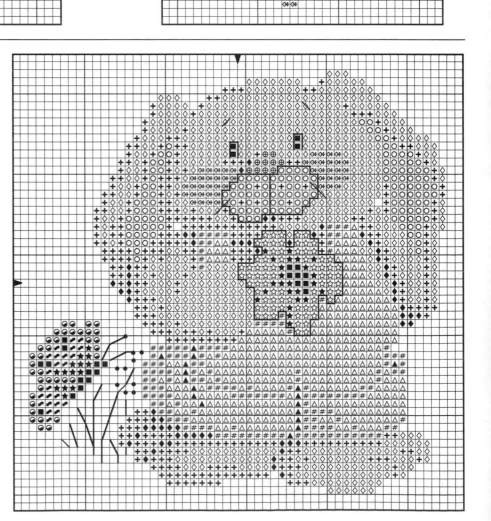

268 Mr. Gander
(40 wide x 51 high)

		Anchor	DMC
▫ =	white	2	blanc
✳ =	orange	329	3340
> =	lt gold	301	744
▫ =	med gold	305	743
◣ =	dk gold	307	783
◇ =	lt blue	975	3753
	med blue	977	3755
♥ =	brown	381	938
	=	Backstitch:		
	bow—dk gold		
	goose—med blue		
	eye—brown		

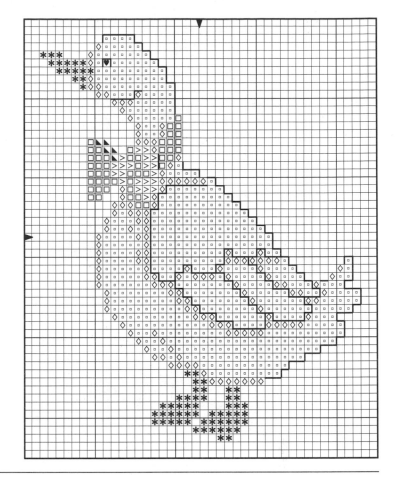

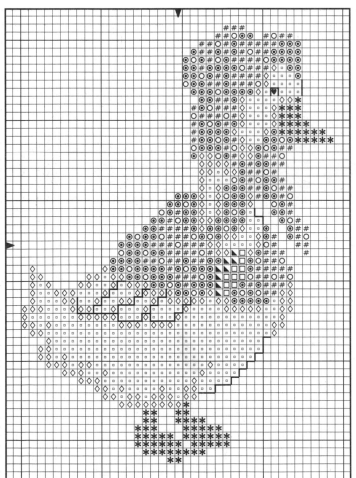

269 Ms. Goose
(39 wide x 55 high)

		Anchor	DMC
▫ =	white	2	blanc
○ =	pink	74	3354
✳ =	orange	329	3340
▫ =	med gold	305	743
◣ =	dk gold	307	783
◇ =	lt blue	975	3753
	med blue	977	334
# =	lt green	214	503
◉ =	med green	217	561
♥ =	brown	381	938
	=	Backstitch: med blue		

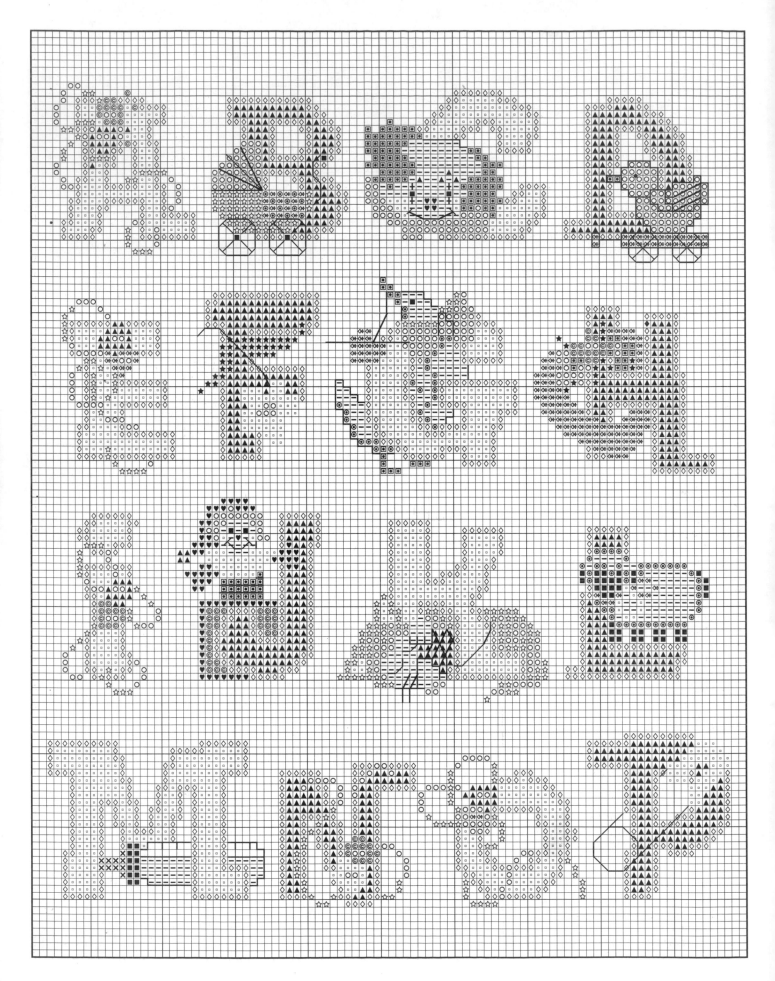

114

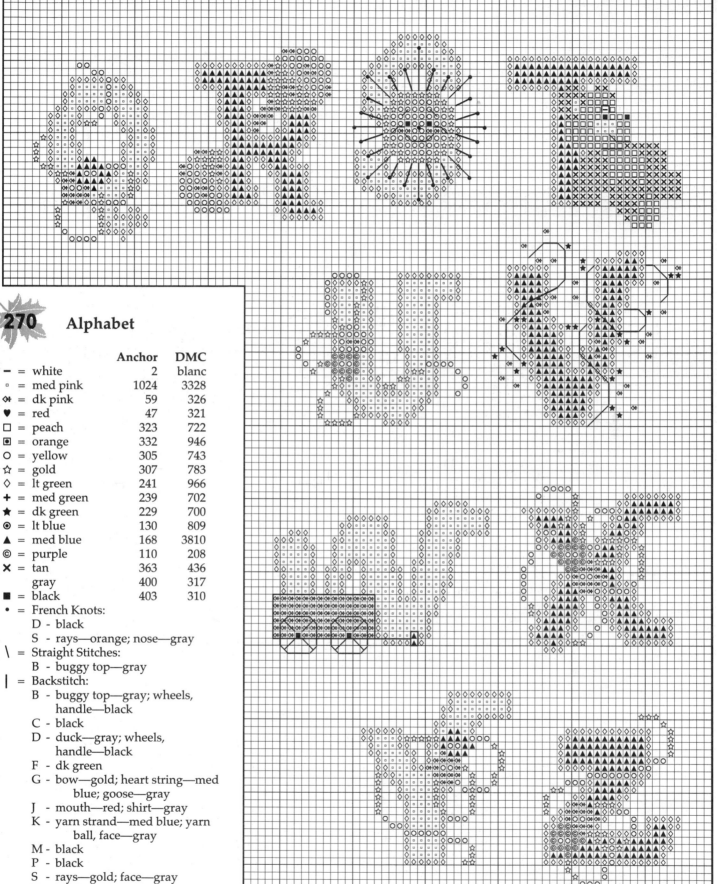

270 Alphabet

		Anchor	DMC
–	= white	2	blanc
▫	= med pink	1024	3328
✢	= dk pink	59	326
♥	= red	47	321
□	= peach	323	722
▣	= orange	332	946
O	= yellow	305	743
☆	= gold	307	783
◇	= lt green	241	966
+	= med green	239	702
★	= dk green	229	700
◉	= lt blue	130	809
▲	= med blue	168	3810
©	= purple	110	208
✕	= tan	363	436
	gray	400	317
■	= black	403	310

• = French Knots:
   D - black
   S - rays—orange; nose—gray
\ = Straight Stitches:
   B - buggy top—gray
| = Backstitch:
   B - buggy top—gray; wheels,
      handle—black
   C - black
   D - duck—gray; wheels,
      handle—black
   F - dk green
   G - bow—gold; heart string—med
      blue; goose—gray
   J - mouth—red; shirt—gray
   K - yarn strand—med blue; yarn
      ball, face—gray
   M - black
   P - black
   S - rays—gold; face—gray
   T - black
   V - dk green
   W - black

271 Country Welcome
(26 wide x 25 high)

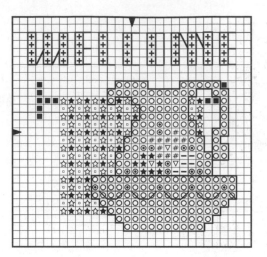

		Anchor	DMC
▫	= white	2	blanc
☆	= lt pink	49	3689
★	= dk pink	66	3688
−	= orange	323	722
▽	= yellow	293	727
◉	= green	242	989
+	= blue	921	931
#	= purple	108	210
O	= tan	942	738
■	= brown	371	433
│	= Backstitch:		

bowl decoration—green
lettering—blue
bowl, pitcher—brown

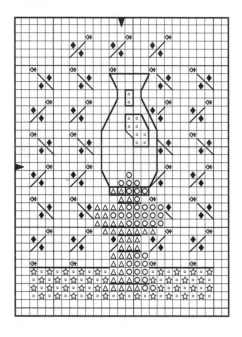

272 Country Glow
(23 wide x 33 high)

		Anchor	DMC
▫	= white	2	blanc
☆	= pink	74	3354
O	= gold	307	783
◆	= lt green	240	368
	med green	242	989
	blue	145	809
✢	= purple	108	210
△	= lt brown	309	781
	dk brown	357	433
│	= Backstitch:		

table edge—pink
wallpaper—med green
lamp chimney—blue
lamp base—dk brown

273 A Rose
(27 wide x 28 high)

		Anchor	DMC
▫	= very lt pink	892	225
◇	= lt pink	24	776
✢	= med pink	76	961
■	= dk pink	42	326
★	= green	257	905
	purple	92	553
	brown	371	433
•	= French Knots: purple		
│	= Backstitch:		

stems—green
rose—brown

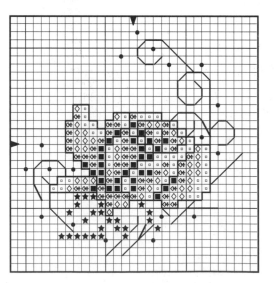

Winter

Winter

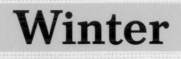

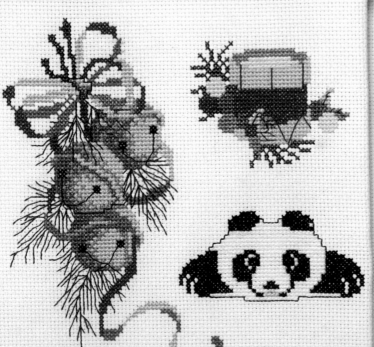

Winter

Winter

120

Winter Design Directory

The charts are in numerical order beginning on page 122.

page 117

page 118

page 119

page 120

274 Stardust
(44 wide x 49 high)

		Anchor	DMC
~ =	lt peach	880	3774
⋎ =	dk peach	778	754
O =	lt turquoise	167	519
⊕ =	med turquoise	169	806
△ =	lt blue	120	3747
▲ =	med blue	122	3807
	orchid	78	3685
⋇ =	med rust	1048	3776
	dk rust	352	300
• =	French Knots: med turquoise		
| =	Backstitch:		
	shirt, bootstraps—med turquoise		
	legs—med blue		
	wings—orchid		
	face—med rust		
	wand—dk rust		
	eyelashes—dk rust (2 strands)		

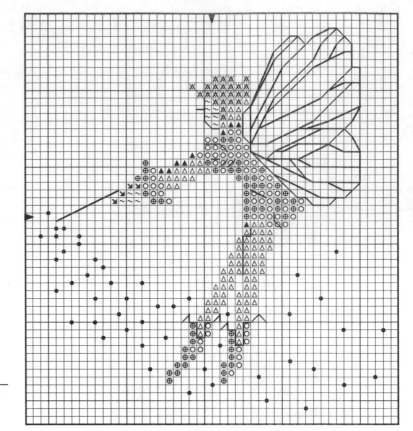

275 Sleighride
(40 wide x 17 high)

		Anchor	DMC
⊕⊹ =	pink	1023	3712
● =	red	19	304
~ =	peach	1011	948
# =	green	208	563
O =	lt blue	9159	828
⁄ =	med blue	978	312
▲ =	dk blue	178	791
^ =	lt brown	373	3828
◉ =	med brown	359	801
✕ =	gray	233	452
■ =	black	403	310
| =	Backstitch:		
	hat, rein—black		
	remaining—gray		

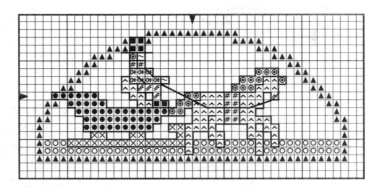

276 Winter Night
(62 wide x 27 high)

		Anchor	DMC
~ =	yellow	301	744
△ =	lt blue	128	800
⊕⊹ =	med blue	121	809
▲ =	dk blue	941	792
| =	Backstitch: med blue		

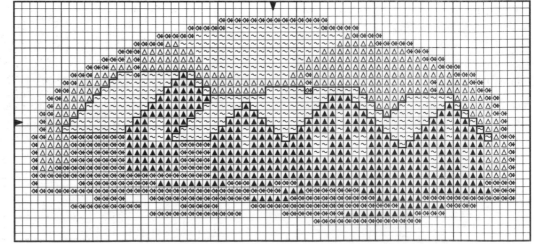

277   Amarylis
(34 wide x 39 high)

		Anchor	DMC
✧	= med red	46	666
⊻	= dk red	47	321
●	= very dk red	44	815
☆	= yellow	891	676
★	= gold	890	729
◇	= lt green	264	3348
#	= med green	266	3347
◆	= dk green	268	469
	gray	236	3799
|	= Backstitch:		
	stamens—yellow		
	veins—gray		

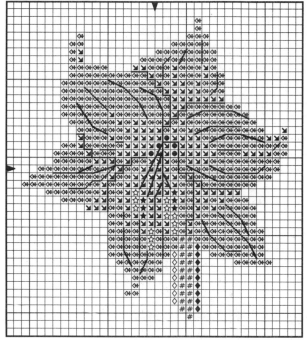

278   Winter Bird
(22 wide x 26 high)

		Anchor	DMC
▫	= white	2	blanc
	green	1044	895
−	= lt rust	1047	402
✗	= med rust	1049	3826
○	= lt gray	398	415
◎	= med gray	400	317
	dk gray	236	3799
■	= black	403	310
•	= French Knot: lt gray		
|	= Backstitch:		
	branch—green		
	bird—dk gray		

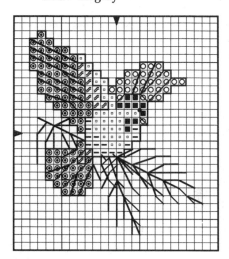

279   Unicorn
(48 wide x 49 high)

		Anchor	DMC
▫	= white	2	blanc
−	= white/filament	2/032	blanc/032
~	= peach	6	754
☆	= yellow	891	676
◆	= green	268	469
○	= lt blue-gray	849	927
	dk blue-gray	922	930
#	= med brown	1007	3772
■	= dk brown	360	898
^	= med gray	231	453
	dk gray	233	452
•	= French Knots: white		
|	= Backstitch:		
	outline of circle—dk blue-gray		
	mane, legs—dk gray		

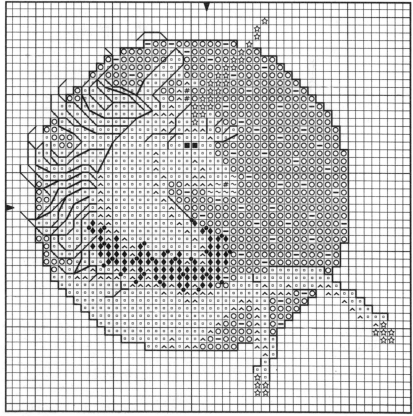

123

280 Leprechaun
(32 wide x 23 high)

		Anchor	DMC
★	= gold	306	783
◇	= lt green	254	3348
◉	= med green	256	704
◆	= dk green	879	500
✕	= brown	358	801
	= Backstitch: brown		

281 Silver Snowflake
(28 wide x 28 high)

Kreinik #8 Braid

silver		001HL
•	= French Knots: silver	
	= Backstitch: silver	

282 Think Snow!
(46 wide x 25 high)

		Anchor	DMC
□	= white	2	blanc
✕	= lt blue	160	827
	med blue	162	517
	dk blue	149	311
•	= French Knot: dk blue		
	= Backstitch:		
	inside of "SNOW "—lt blue		
	"SNOW !" outline—med blue		
	"think"—dk blue		

283 Winter Mill Stream
(52 wide x 29 high)

		Anchor	DMC
□	= white	2	blanc
○	= lt rose	1013	3778
✕	= med rose	1014	355
●	= dk rose	1015	3777
#	= green	859	523
~	= blue	158	747
✐	= rust	351	400
∧	= lt gray	231	453
◉	= med gray	233	452
	dk gray	236	3799
•	= French Knot: dk gray		
	= Backstitch:		
	door and window outlines, paddles		
	on paddlewheel—white		
	paddlewheel spokes—lt rose		
	tree—rust		

house, stone wall, door center—dk gray

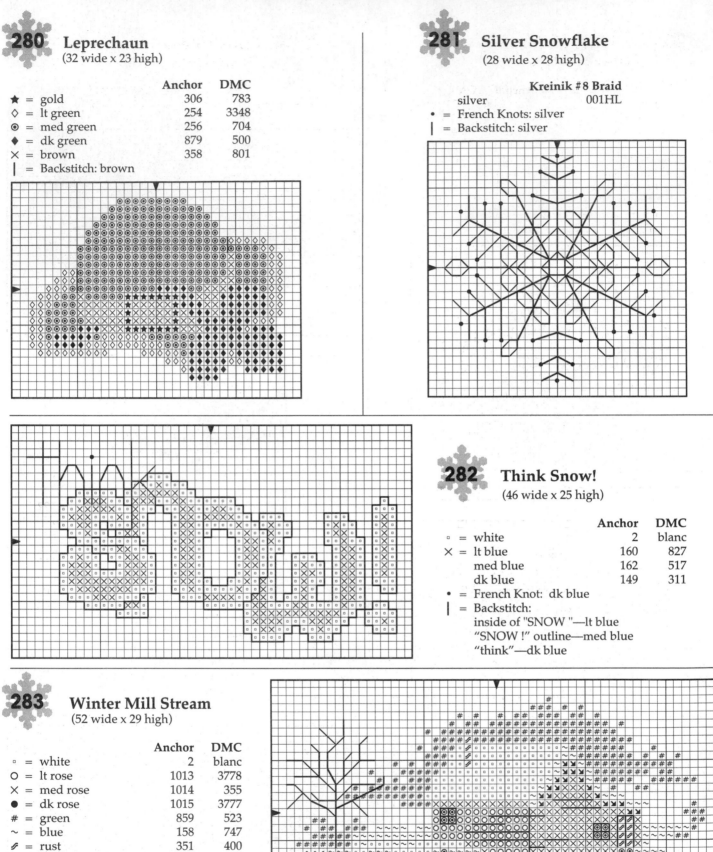

124

284 I Love Basketball
(34 wide x 26 high)

		Anchor	DMC
	red	47	321
▲ =	orange	324	721
	brown	379	840
	med brown	936	632
■ =	dk brown	359	801
	=	Backstitch:		
	heart outline—red		
	"I"—lt brown		
	rim & net—med brown		
	"BASKETBALL"—dk brown		

285 Nordic Scene
(40 wide x 22 high)

		Anchor	DMC
× =	green	845	730

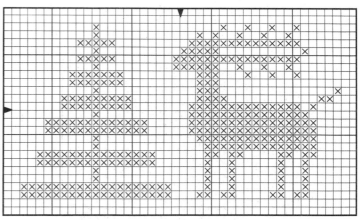

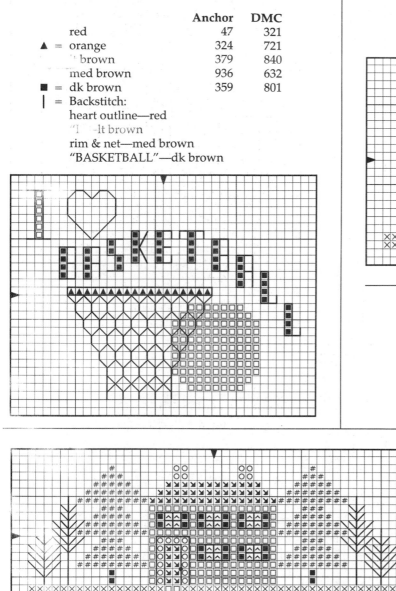

286 Winter Manor
(46 wide x 18 high)

		Anchor	DMC
	cream	275	746
○ =	lt red	1027	3722
↘ =	dk red	1015	3777
# =	yellow-green	844	3012
	blue-green	683	890
× =	blue	975	3753
□ =	lt brown	369	435
■ =	dk brown	358	801
^ =	gray	234	762
• =	French Knot: dk brown		
	=	Backstitch:		
	inner door line—cream		
	trees—blue-green		
	windowpanes, shutters, door		
	frame—dk brown		

287 Moonrise
(44 wide x 27 high)

		Anchor	DMC
▫ =	white	2	blanc
~ =	yellow	292	3078
◆ =	green	246	986
✛ =	blue	160	827
• =	French Knots: yellow		
	=	Backstitch: blue		

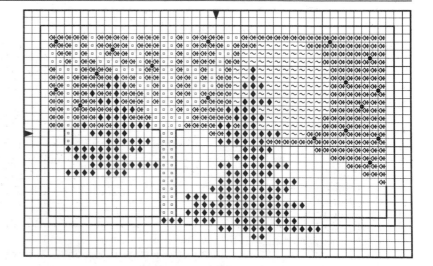

288 Santa Elf (22 wide x 48 high)

		Anchor	DMC
▫ =	white	2	blanc
~ =	peach	880	3774
☆ =	yellow	386	3823
♦ =	green	243	703
■ =	brown	944	434
● =	gray	399	318
❘ =	Backstitch: gray		

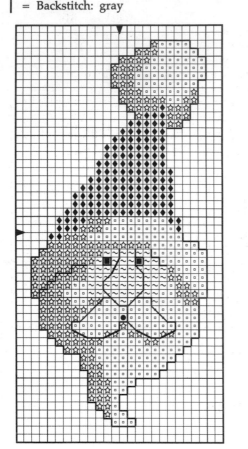

290 Cupid Angel (39 wide x 23 high)

		Anchor	DMC
~ =	lt pink	271	819
✤ =	med lt pink	23	3713
	med pink	25	3326
◉ =	med rose	77	3687
	dk rose	65	3685
☆ =	lt yellow	293	727
★ =	med yellow	305	743
	dk yellow	306	783
♦ =	green	923	3818
☐ =	lt brown	369	435
■ =	dk brown	380	838
⌀ =	gray	400	317
• =	French Knots:		
	scattered with roses—dk rose		
	bow ends—dk brown		
	eyes, mouth—gray		
❘ =	Backstitch:		
	leg, arm, face—med pink		
	hearts, roses—dk rose	bow, hair—dk brown	
	wings—dk yellow	arrow, eyes—gray	

289 Winter Goose (40 wide x 47 high)

		Anchor	DMC
▫ =	white	2	blanc
✕ =	med blue	175	809
● =	dk blue	177	792
~ =	tan	942	738
△ =	lt brown	376	3774
▲ =	dk brown	379	840
⌃ =	lt gray	398	415
◉ =	med gray	235	414
■ =	dk gray	236	3799
❘ =	Backstitch:		
	eye—white		
	border—med blue		
	white areas—lt gray		
	feathers, nostril—dk gray		

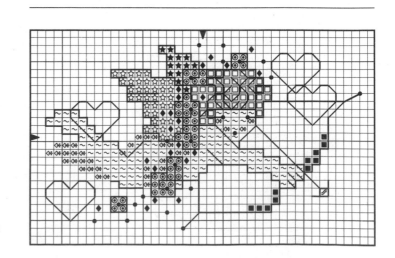

291 Ice Hockey (18 wide x 34 high)

		Anchor	DMC
✿	= med red	1027	3722
●	= dk red	44	815
+	= brown	379	840
■	= black	403	310
		= Backstitch:		

"ICE"—med red
"HOCKEY"—dk red
puck—black

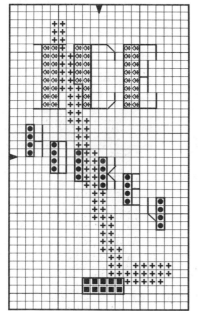

292 Jolly Snowman (32 wide x 24 high)

		Anchor	DMC
▫	= white	2	blanc
✿	= med red	46	666
♥	= dk red	22	814
▲	= orange	324	721
◇	= lt green	203	564
◆	= dk green	923	3818
O	= blue	343	3752
■	= black	403	310
•	= French Knots: white		
		= Backstitch:		

pipe bowl—white
hat brim, eyes, eyelashes, mouth, pipe stem,
chin, nose—black

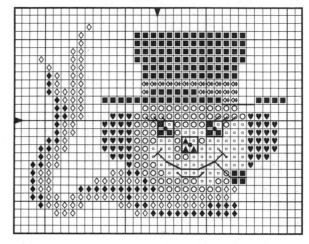

293 Holly Sprig (25 wide x 20 high)

		Anchor	DMC
O	= lt red	1023	3712
✿	= med red	9046	321
●	= dk red	20	815
◇	= lt green	1043	369
#	= med green	859	523
◆	= dk green	1044	895
		= Backstitch: dk green		

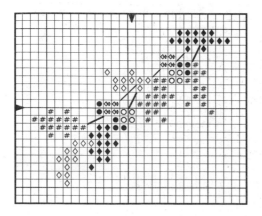

294 Homeward Bound (26 wide x 22 high)

		Anchor	DMC
▫	= white	2	blanc
~	= blue	343	3752
O	= lt taupe	830	644
✕	= med taupe	903	640
●	= dk taupe	905	3021
▧	= gray	400	317
■	= black	403	310
		= Backstitch:		

wings—gray
beneath and around eye—black

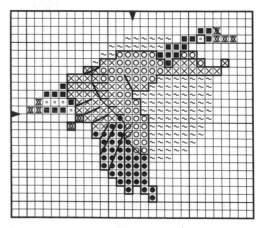

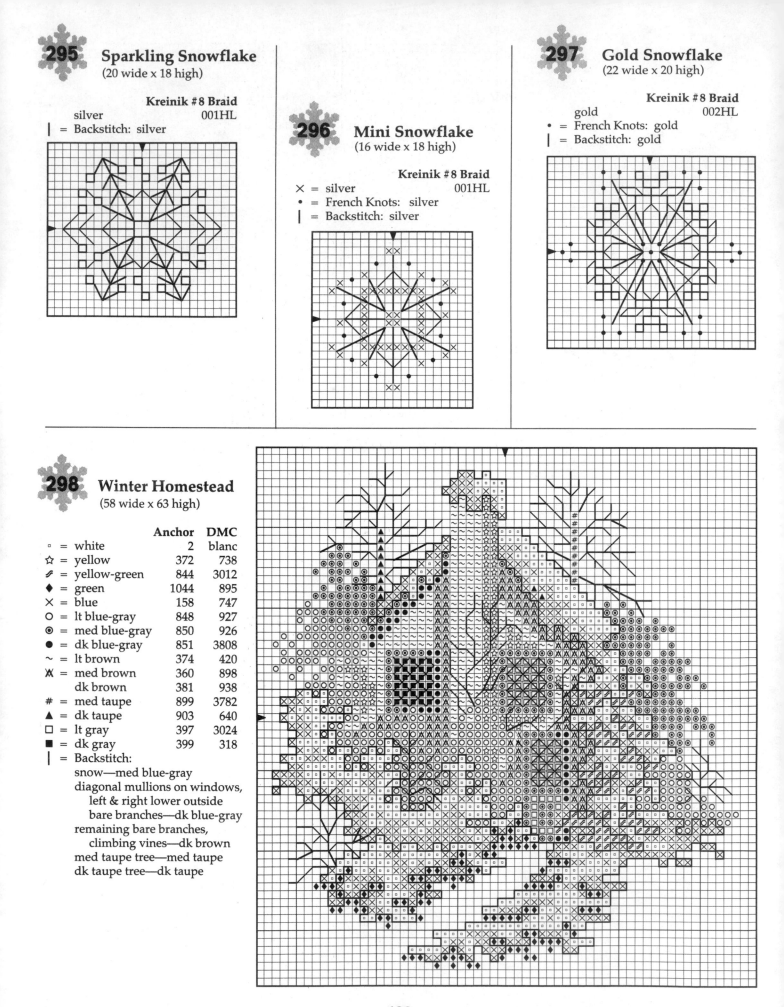

295 **Sparkling Snowflake**
(20 wide x 18 high)

Kreinik #8 Braid
silver   001HL
| = Backstitch: silver

296 **Mini Snowflake**
(16 wide x 18 high)

Kreinik #8 Braid
× = silver   001HL
• = French Knots: silver
| = Backstitch: silver

297 **Gold Snowflake**
(22 wide x 20 high)

Kreinik #8 Braid
gold   002HL
• = French Knots: gold
| = Backstitch: gold

298 **Winter Homestead**
(58 wide x 63 high)

		Anchor	DMC
▫ =	white	2	blanc
☆ =	yellow	372	738
✎ =	yellow-green	844	3012
◆ =	green	1044	895
× =	blue	158	747
○ =	lt blue-gray	848	927
◉ =	med blue-gray	850	926
● =	dk blue-gray	851	3808
~ =	lt brown	374	420
⋈ =	med brown	360	898
	dk brown	381	938
# =	med taupe	899	3782
▲ =	dk taupe	903	640
□ =	lt gray	397	3024
■ =	dk gray	399	318

| = Backstitch:
  snow—med blue-gray
  diagonal mullions on windows,
    left & right lower outside
    bare branches—dk blue-gray
  remaining bare branches,
    climbing vines—dk brown
  med taupe tree—med taupe
  dk taupe tree—dk taupe

128

299 Winter Fairy
(55 wide x 99 high)

Note: For wings, use two strands of floss and one strand of pearl (032) blending filament.

		Anchor	DMC
▫	= white/filament	2/032	blanc/032
O	= lt pink/filament	24/032	963/032
♥	= med pink	68	3687
~	= lt peach	1011	948
◉	= med peach	881	945
	dk peach	914	407
☆	= yellow/filament	891/032	676/032
◇	= green/filament	203/032	564/032
✪	= med blue	976	3752
	dk blue	979	312
△	= lt brown	368	437
⌀	= med brown	370	434
	dk brown	359	801
│	= Backstitch:		

mouth—med pink
fingers, leg, chin—dk peach
dress—dk blue
hair, eyes—dk brown

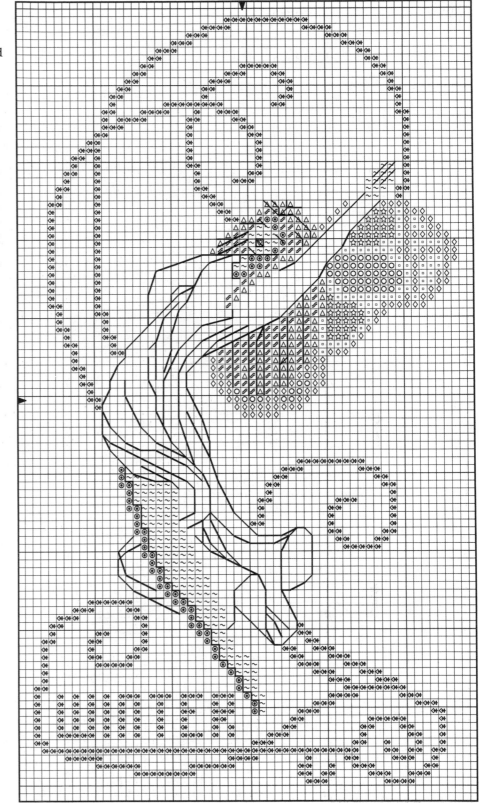

300 Mini Wreath
(13 wide x 14 high)

		Anchor	DMC
●	= red	47	321
✳	= orange	316	970
☆	= yellow	291	444
◆	= green	226	703
⋈	= blue	133	820
│	= Backstitch: red		

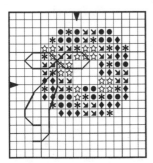

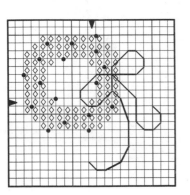

301 Berry Wreath
(17 wide x 17 high)

		Anchor	DMC		
	red	1006	304	●	= French Knots: red
◇	= lt green	266	3347	│	= Backstitch: dk green
	dk green	1044	895		

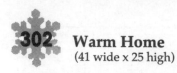

302 Warm Home
(41 wide x 25 high)

		Anchor	DMC
	med rose	69	3687
	dk rose	70	902
# =	med green	215	320
	dk green	218	319
⊕ =	blue	921	931
	brown	352	300

⬎ = Lazy Daisies: med green
• = French Knot: dk green
| = Backstitch:
"warm"—med rose
hearts—dk rose
"Friends," leaves—dk green
remaining lettering—brown

303 Cozy Cap
(28 wide x 23 high)

		Anchor	DMC
▫ =	white	2	blanc
○ =	lt rose	969	316
⊕ =	med rose	972	3803
~ =	peach	9575	3830
◇ =	lt green	260	772
◆ =	dk green	262	3363
✕ =	blue	158	747
	gray	236	3799

• = French Knots:
polka dots—med rose
eye—gray
| = Backstitch: gray

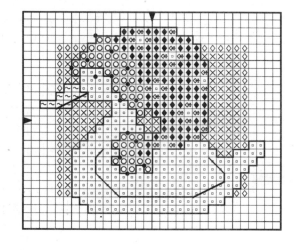

304 Cuddling Time
(44 wide x 39 high)

		Anchor	DMC
▫ =	white	2	blanc
☆ =	lt pink	48	3689
⊕ =	med pink	55	957
★ =	dk pink	57	602
✎ =	very dk pink	896	3721
	turquoise	169	806
○ =	lt blue	121	809
⊕ =	med blue	122	3807
~ =	very lt brown	367	738
♡ =	lt brown	369	435
# =	med brown	371	434
♥ =	dk brown	360	898
▲ =	very dk brown	382	3371
∧ =	gray	234	762
■ =	black	403	310

| = Backstitch:
lettering—turquoise
eyebrows, mouths—very dk brown
eyes—black

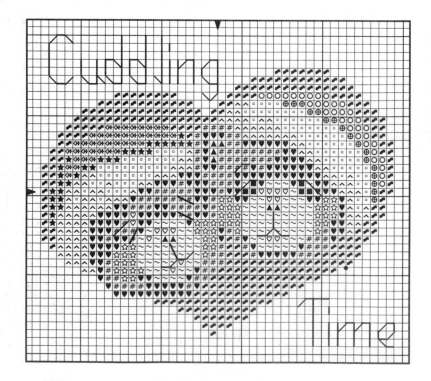

305 Frozen Forest
(78 wide x 40 high)

		Anchor	DMC
△ =	lt turquoise	167	519
✦ =	med turquoise	168	3810
▲ =	dk turquoise	170	3765

| = Backstitch:
    inside border, two trees on each side—med turquoise
    outside border, center tree—dk turquoise

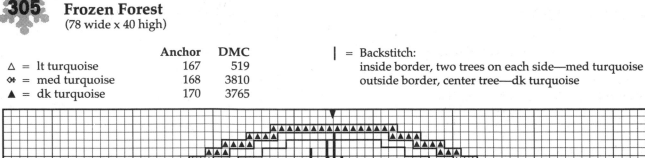

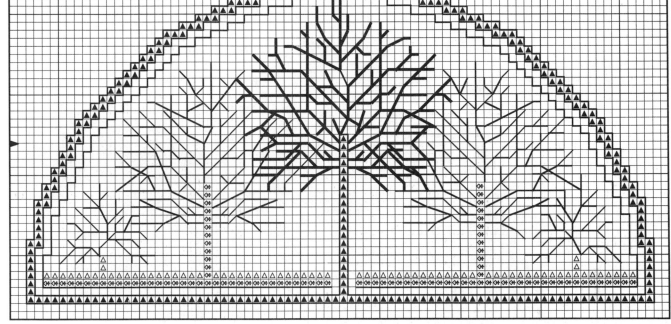

306 Cozy Quarters
(54 wide x 53 high)

		Anchor	DMC
▫ =	white	2	blanc
+ =	orange	324	721
◇ =	lt green	213	504
# =	med green	216	502
◆ =	dk green	218	319
∅ =	lt turquoise	928	3811
∅ =	med turquoise	433	996
● =	blue	164	824
✕ =	lt blue-gray	1037	3756
✦ =	med blue-gray	1032	3752
~ =	very lt rust	366	951
⊥ =	lt rust	368	437
△ =	lt brown	369	435
▲ =	med brown	358	801
⬕ =	very dk brown	360	898
⧓ =	lt gray	399	318
	med gray	235	414
■ =	dk gray	236	3799

| = Backstitch:
    hat, scarf—dk green
    front of birdhouse—med brown
    side of birdhouse—very dk brown
    smoke, branches, beak,
        snow—lt gray
    bird, hanging chain—med gray
    chimney—dk gray

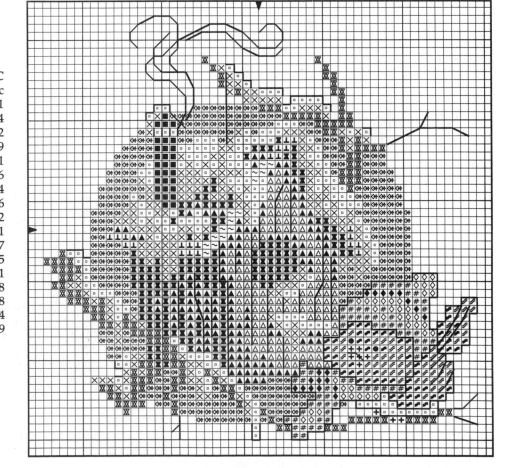

307 Golden Manse
(31 wide x 31 high)

		Anchor	DMC
☆ =	yellow	891	676
◇ =	lt yellow-green	278	3819
# =	med yellow-green	281	732
◆ =	green	263	3362
~ =	blue-gray	158	747
✿ =	med blue	128	800
▲ =	dk blue	133	820
^ =	tan	368	437
◉ =	rust	1004	920
	gray	400	317

| = Backstitch:
latticework—med yellow-green
windows, tower turret, fretwork above and
   below windows, door—dk blue
roof, steps—gray

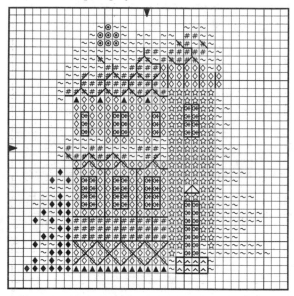

308 Painted Lady
(33 wide x 24 high)

		Anchor	DMC
▫ =	cream	275	746
○ =	lt pink	271	819
✿ =	med pink	24	963
● =	dk pink	38	961
✖ =	very dk pink	39	309
◆ =	green	212	561
~ =	blue	158	747
✕ =	purple	103	211
✖ =	med brown	379	840
	dk brown	936	632

| = Backstitch:
center dormer—med pink
windows—dk pink
door—very dk pink
side dormer roofs, steps—dk brown

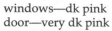

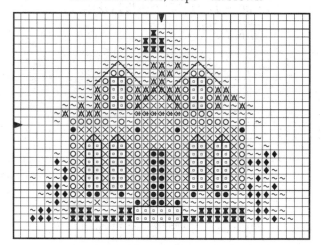

309 Winter Castle
(39 wide x 41 high)

		Anchor	DMC
~ =	blue	158	747
✎ =	blue-gray	921	931
◇ =	med green	267	469
◆ =	dk green	862	520
○ =	lt brown	376	3774
© =	med brown	379	840
● =	dk brown	936	632
^ =	lt rust	336	758
✿ =	med rust	337	3776
✘ =	dk rust	339	920
□ =	lt gray	397	3024
✕ =	med gray	399	318
■ =	dk gray	400	317

| = Backstitch:
brown stonework, door—dk brown
windows—lt gray
rust & gray stonework—dk gray

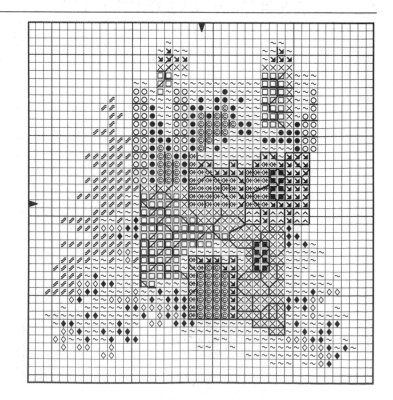

 **310** **Classic Comfort**
(38 wide x 31 high)

		Anchor	DMC
▫	= white	2	blanc
○	= lt pink	1021	761
	med pink	1025	347
●	= red	1015	3777
✕	= orange	328	3341
◆	= green	1044	895
~	= blue-gray	158	747
□	= lt brown	1008	3773
#	= med brown	1007	3772
	dk brown	936	632
◉	= rust	341	918
⋈	= gray	235	414
|	= Backstitch:		

inside fan window—white
roof line—med pink
trim, windows, door—dk brown
steps—rust
chimneys—gray

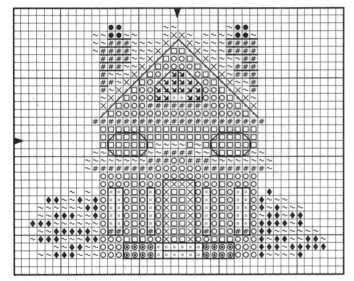

 311 **Mississippi Manor**
(31 wide x 31 high)

		Anchor	DMC
▫	= cream	275	746
☆	= orange	336	758
◆	= green	210	562
~	= blue-gray	158	747
♡	= lt purple	342	211
#	= med purple	109	209
♥	= dk purple	112	552
⋈	= brown	358	801
◉	= rust	355	975
+	= lt gray	398	415
	dk gray	236	3799
|	= Backstitch:		

door frame—med purple
windows, railing, door—dk purple
steps—brown
roof—dk gray

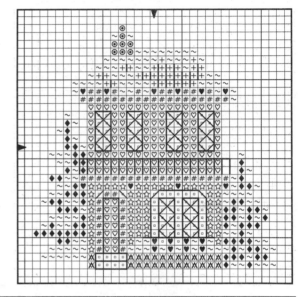

 312 **First Snow**
(42 wide x 40 high)

		Anchor	DMC
▫	= white	2	blanc
◆	= green	217	561
~	= lt blue-gray	848	927
✕	= med blue-gray	921	931
○	= very lt brown	367	738
∧	= lt brown	369	435
#	= med brown	371	434
⋈	= dk brown	360	898
✗	= very dk brown	382	3371
■	= black	403	310
•	= French Knots: white		
|	= Backstitch:		

top of head, legs—med brown
ears—dk brown
eyebrow, eye—very dk brown
mouth—black

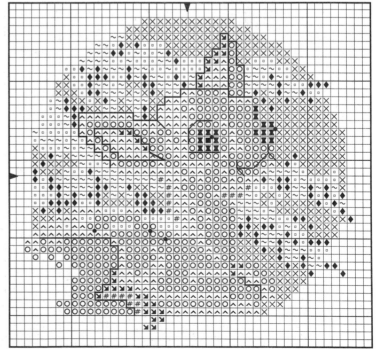

313 Winter Warmth
(28 wide x 39 high)

		Anchor	DMC
▫ =	white	2	blanc
❀ =	pink	52	957
✕ =	yellow-green	268	469
◆ =	green	878	501
~ =	lt blue-gray	158	747
◢ =	dk blue-gray	920	932
◿ =	med brown	944	434
▲ =	dk brown	1050	3781
◉ =	rust	370	434
✖ =	med gray	1041	844
■ =	very dk gray	236	3799
⎮ =	Backstitch:		
	roof over front door, smoke—med gray		
	brick path—very dk gray		

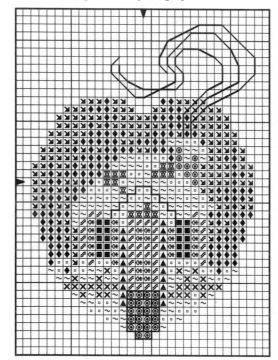

314 Raccoon
(36 wide x 32 high)

		Anchor	DMC
▫ =	white	2	blanc
~ =	lt blue-gray	158	747
✕ =	med blue-gray	849	927
╱ =	very lt brown	372	738
○ =	lt brown	368	437
+ =	med brown	369	435
◉ =	med dk brown	358	801
◢ =	dk brown	360	898
✖ =	very dk brown	381	938
✖ =	gray	400	317
■ =	black	403	310
⎮ =	Backstitch:		
	eyes, face—white		
	branches—gray		

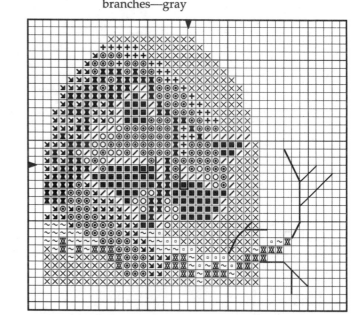

315 A True Blue Friend
(46 wide x 40 high)

		Anchor	DMC
▫ =	white	2	blanc
≃ =	pink	25	3326
♥ =	red	1014	355
◆ =	green	212	561
➴ =	turquoise	187	958
❀ =	lt blue	158	747
✕ =	med blue	162	517
	dk blue	133	820
	blue-gray	922	930
■ =	black	403	310
• =	French Knot: dk blue		
⎮ =	Backstitch:		
	lettering—dk blue		
	face, sleeve—blue-gray		
	mouth, scarf, eyes, nose—black		

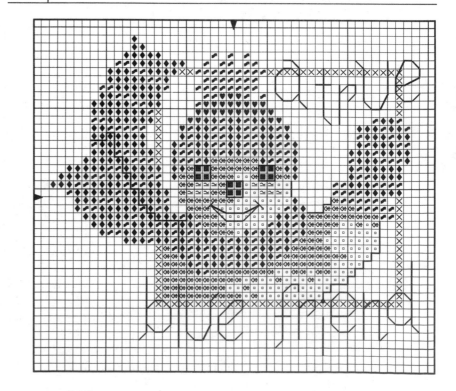

316 Bowling
(38 wide x 44 high)

		Anchor	DMC
▫	= white	2	blanc
~	= cream	885	739
O	= lt red	10	351
◉	= med red	47	321
	med gray	232	453
	dk gray	400	317
■	= black	403	310
		= Backstitch:		
	bowling ball—white		
	pins—med gray		
	motion lines—dk gray		

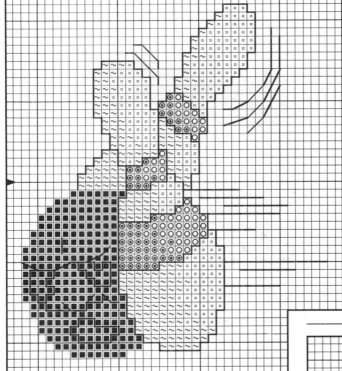

317 Winter Joy
(37 wide x 31 high)

		Anchor	DMC
▫	= white	2	blanc
✕	= pink	10	351
♡	= lt blue	175	809
♥	= dk blue	177	792
	brown	359	801
∧	= lt gray	232	453
⊠	= med gray	400	317
■	= black	403	310
•	= French Knots: pink		
		= Backstitch:		
	wing top—dk blue		
	branches—brown		
	neck feathers—med gray		
	topknot, eye, beak—black		

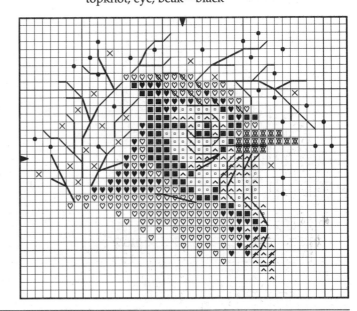

318 Cardinal
(47 wide x 42 high)

		Anchor	DMC
▫	= white	2	blanc
O	= lt red	1024	3328
◉	= med red	47	321
~	= blue-gray	9159	828
◇	= lt green	259	772
#	= med green	261	989
♦	= dk green	263	3362
■	= black	403	310
		= Backstitch:		
	eye (except extension)—white		
	remaining eye, beak, feathers—black		

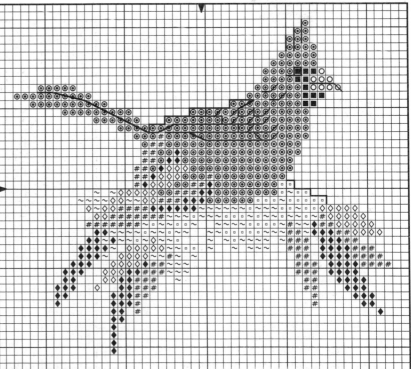

319 Ski Time
(48 wide x 41 high)

		Anchor	DMC
▫ =	white	2	blanc
○ =	lt blue-gray	274	927
● =	dk blue-gray	850	926
ǀ =	Backstitch:		
	skier (except face)—white		
	poles, face—dk blue-gray		

320 I Love Winter
(74 wide x 6 high)

		Anchor	DMC
	red	1006	304
✦ =	blue	162	517
	med brown	357	433
✦ =	dk brown	360	898
• =	French Knots: med brown		
ǀ =	Backstitch:		
	heart—red		
	"E," "R"—blue		
	tracery—med brown		
	"I"—dk brown		

321 Snow Angel
(50 wide x 37 high)

		Anchor	DMC
▫ =	white	2	blanc
	pink	54	956
~ =	lt peach	1010	951
	dk peach	1008	3773
○ =	lt turquoise	158	747
⊕ =	med turquoise	168	3810
⊾ =	dk turquoise	169	806
◥ =	very dk turquoise	170	3765
⦰ =	med blue	161	813
∧ =	med brown	379	840
■ =	dk brown	936	632
	Kreinik #8 Braid		
	turquoise		006
• =	French Knots:		
	mouth—pink		
	snowflakes, sparkles—turquoise braid		
ǀ =	Backstitch:		
	heart—pink		
	face, hands—dk peach		
	snowflakes—turquoise braid		
	lettering—dk turquoise		
	wings—med blue		
	eyes—dk brown		

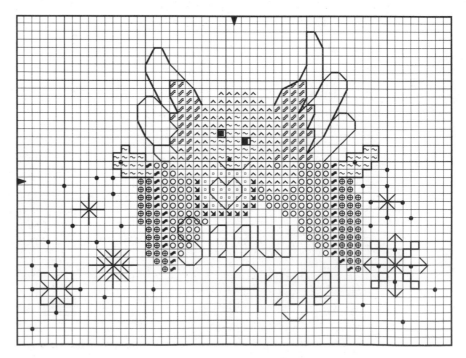

322 Snow Place Like Home
(56 wide x 36 high)

		Anchor	DMC
□	= white	2	blanc
✧	= pink	60	605
♥	= red	1014	355
♦	= green	210	562
~	= lt blue	158	747
	med blue	161	813
⋈	= dk blue	162	517
⊙	= rust	369	435
■	= black	403	310

• = French Knots:
buds—pink
tracery—dk blue

| = Backstitch:
windows, blue background—white
stems—green
lettering—med blue
tracery—dk blue

323 Lighthouse
(39 wide x 37 high)

		Anchor	DMC
□	= white	2	blanc
O	= lt red	895	223
⊕	= med red	897	221
●	= dk red	45	814
+	= yellow	300	745
−	= very lt gold	361	738
☆	= lt gold	363	436
∞	= med gold	365	435
★	= dk gold	309	781
◇	= lt yellow-green	842	3013
#	= med yellow-green	844	3012
♦	= dk yellow-green	846	3011
T	= green	217	561
~	= lt blue-gray	847	3072
⋈	= dk blue-gray	920	932
∧	= tan	367	738
■	= gray	236	3799

| = Backstitch:
water—green
background forest—dk blue-gray
lighthouse—gray

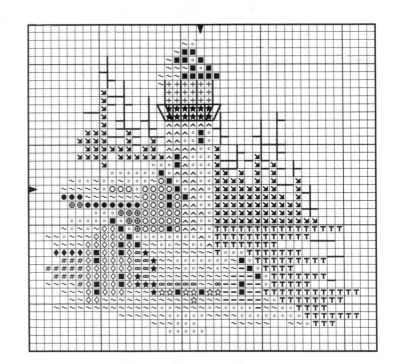

137

324 Someone To Love
(26 wide x 24 high)

		Anchor	DMC
−	= cream	926	ecru
✎	= red	47	304
+	= blue	121	809
◇	= rust	349	301
✕	= brown	889	610
▲	= black	403	310
•	= French Knots: rust		
│	= Backstitch:		
	"E"—blue		
	feet—rust		
	remaining lettering—brown		
	nose, eyes—black		

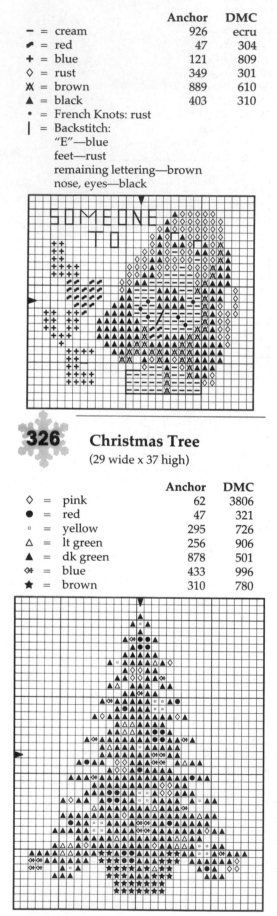

325 Joy
(35 wide x 32 high)

		Anchor	DMC
+	= med red	35	3801
	dk red	47	304
▫	= gold	306	725
☆	= lt green	238	703
	dk green	229	700
│	= Backstitch:		
	"JOY"—dk red		
	branches—dk green		

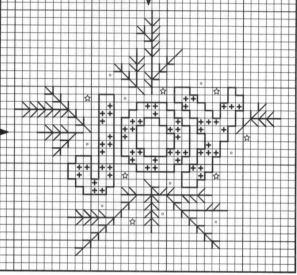

326 Christmas Tree
(29 wide x 37 high)

		Anchor	DMC
◇	= pink	62	3806
●	= red	47	321
▫	= yellow	295	726
△	= lt green	256	906
▲	= dk green	878	501
✧	= blue	433	996
★	= brown	310	780

327 Candle Wreath
(27 wide x 27 high)

		Anchor	DMC
◇	= pink	75	962
●	= red	47	321
△	= orange	330	947
▫	= yellow	295	726
+	= lt green	256	906
▼	= dk green	258	904
☆	= blue	433	996
	brown	357	433
│	= Backstitch:		
	flame—orange		
	wick—brown		

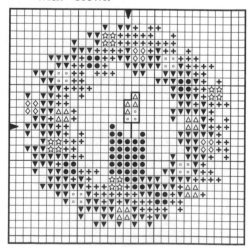

328 Poinsettia
(27 wide x 27 high)

		Anchor	DMC
+	= red	47	304
O	= yellow	306	725
✤	= green	257	905
◆	= blue	921	931
|	= Backstitch: blue		

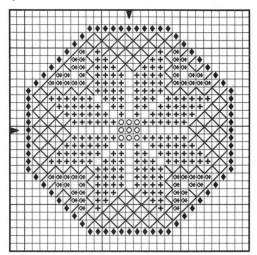

330 Christmas Stocking
(22 wide x 33 high)

		Anchor	DMC
−	= white	2	blanc
☆	= med red	46	666
✄	= dk red	47	304
▽	= orange	333	608
O	= yellow	297	973
◇	= lt green	255	907
◆	= dk green	258	904
▲	= purple	110	208
	brown	357	433
•	= French Knots: med red		
|	= Backstitch:		
	branches—dk green		
	fruit, leaves, stocking—brown		

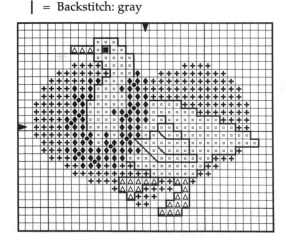

329 Christmas Candle
(26 wide x 34 high)

		Anchor	DMC
	lt red	11	351
+	= med red	35	3801
O	= yellow	306	725
▽	= med green	267	469
■	= dk green	246	986
◇	= lt blue	920	932
▼	= dk blue	922	930
	brown	357	433
•	= French Knots: lt red		
|	= Backstitch: brown		

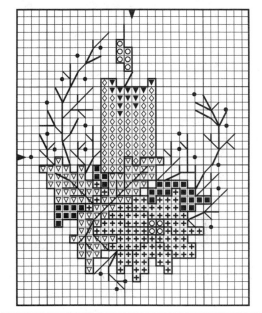

331 Christmas Goose
(29 wide x 23 high)

		Anchor	DMC
▫	= white	2	blanc
+	= red (1 strand)	1006	304
△	= orange	328	3341
◆	= green	258	904
■	= gray	401	413
•	= French Knots: red		
|	= Backstitch: gray		

332 Country Man
(22 wide x 28 high)

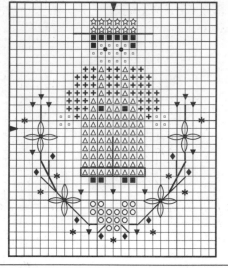

		Anchor	DMC
O	= pink	66	3688
▫	= peach	778	754
◇	= gold	307	783
◆	= green	242	989
+	= blue	145	809
	purple	111	553
△	= lt brown	309	781
■	= dk brown	357	433

◌ = Lazy Daisy:
  upper flowers—pink
  lower flowers—blue
French Knots:
✱ = flower dots—pink
▼ = flower dots—purple
• = eyes—dk brown
| = Backstitch:
  hat—gold
  stems—green
  pants—dk brown

333 Country Woman
(22 wide x 28 high)

		Anchor	DMC
~	= white	1	blanc
O	= pink	66	3688
★	= rose	42	309
▫	= peach	778	754
◇	= yellow	297	973
◆	= green	242	989
	blue	145	809
	purple	111	553
	lt brown	309	781
■	= dk brown	357	433

◌ = Lazy Daisy:
  upper flowers—pink
  lower flowers—blue
French Knots:
✱ = flower dots—pink
▼ = flower dots—purple
• = eyes—dk brown
| = Backstitch:
  stems—green
  hair—lt brown

334 Holiday Lantern
(30 wide x 31 high)

		Anchor	DMC
–	= white	2	blanc
✱	= med red	47	304
♥	= dk red	44	814
+	= med orange	316	970
▲	= dk orange	335	606
▫	= lt yellow	300	745
◇	= med yellow	297	973
◢	= dk yellow	303	742
⊟	= med green	256	906
●	= dk green	258	904
O	= lt blue	159	3325
◉	= med blue	161	826
■	= gray	401	413

| = Backstitch:
  flame, berries—dk red
  branches, leaves—dk green
  snow—med blue

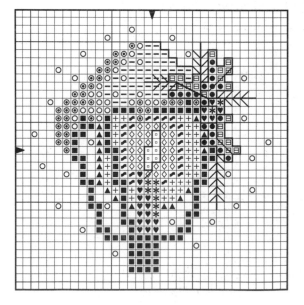

335 Home For Christmas
(37 wide x 38 high)

		Anchor	DMC
−	= white	2	blanc
●	= red	44	815
▫	= yellow	306	725
▲	= green	243	988
◇	= blue	159	3325
☆	= lt gray-blue	921	931
■	= dk gray-blue	149	311
	brown	360	898
	gray	399	318
│	= Backstitch:		

"Home," "Christmas"—red
"For," trees—green
snow—lt gray-blue
house—brown
smoke—gray

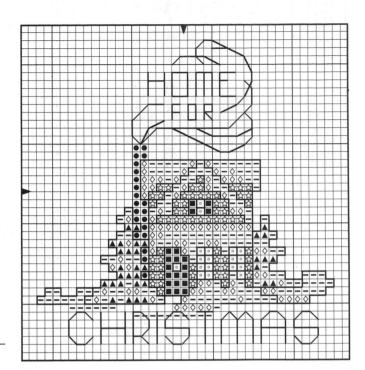

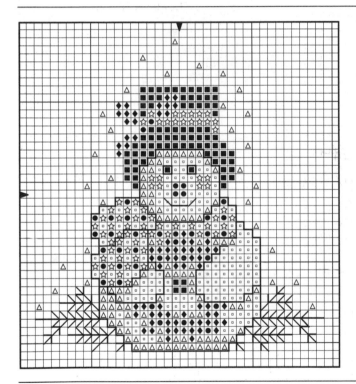

336 Holiday Snowman
(36 wide x 39 high)

		Anchor	DMC
▫	= white	2	blanc
☆	= pink	40	956
●	= red	47	304
◆	= green	258	904
△	= blue	167	519
■	= gray	401	413
│	= Backstitch:		

branches—green
snowman, mouth, eyes, scarf—gray

337 Christmas Music
(28 wide x 22 high)

		Anchor	DMC
☆	= lt red	42	309
+	= dk red	47	321
◣	= orange	333	608
▫	= yellow	297	973
◆	= gold	307	783
◇	= lt green	255	907
■	= dk green	258	904
△	= purple	110	208
	brown	357	433
│	= Backstitch:		

branches—dk green
remaining—brown

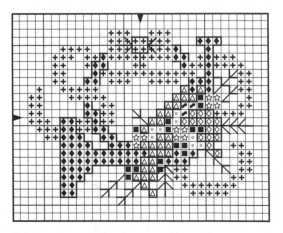

141

338 Della Robbia Wreath
(45 wide x 58 high)

		Anchor	DMC
O	= lt pink	48	3689
+	= med pink	74	3354
▲	= dk pink	42	326
▫	= lt red	50	957
◇	= med red	47	321
⊙	= dk red	20	815
●	= very dk red	44	814
△	= lt orange	323	722
✢	= med orange	326	720
□	= lt yellow	293	727
©	= med yellow	306	725
✳	= gold	308	782
–	= very lt yellow-green	264	772
◈	= lt yellow-green	265	3348
⋈	= med yellow-green	257	905
◆	= dk yellow-green	267	469
♥	= very dk yellow-green	269	936
#	= med green	217	367
★	= dk green	246	986
∧	= lt brown	362	437
☆	= med brown	309	781
■	= dk brown	357	433

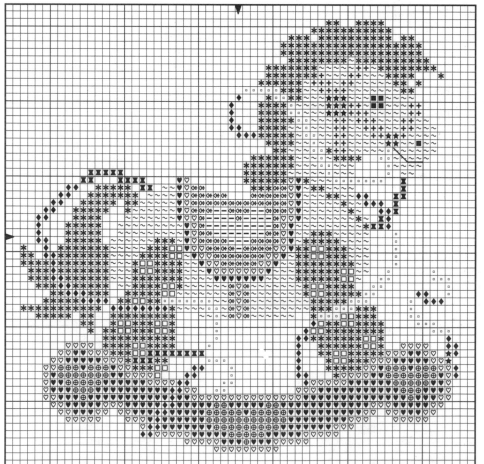

339 Rocking Horse
(59 wide x 58 high)

		Anchor	DMC
–	= lt pink	55	604
⊕	= med pink	57	602
★	= gold	306	725
+	= green	203	954
♡	= lt blue	9159	3761
✢	= med blue	161	813
♥	= dk blue	162	517
~	= lt purple	108	210
*	= med purple	110	208
▫	= lt rust	336	402
◆	= med rust	338	922
⋈	= dk rust	5975	356
□	= tan	880	3774
■	= brown	359	801
|	= Backstitch: brown		

142

340 Jingle Bells
(56 wide x 91 high)

		Anchor	DMC
□	= lt pink	24	776
✢	= med pink	27	899
●	= dk pink	42	309
▫	= lt gold	361	738
◇	= med gold	397	3024
◆	= dk gold	307	783
◞	= green	878	501
■	= brown	381	938
|	= Backstitch:		
	branches—green		
	bells, bow—brown		

341 Toy Soldier
(12 wide x 31 high)

		Anchor	DMC
▫	= white	2	blanc
✢	= lt pink	50	957
▲	= dk pink	59	326
☆	= gold	307	783
+	= blue	978	312
~	= tan	4146	950
■	= gray	236	3799
•	= French Knots: gray		
|	= Backstitch: gray		

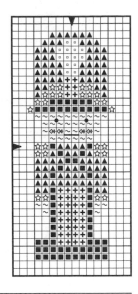

342 Santa Claus
(18 wide x 38 high)

		Anchor	DMC
▫	= white	2	blanc
−	= peach	778	754
◇	= pink	74	3354
✢	= med red	47	321
▲	= dk red	20	498
☆	= gold	306	725
◆	= green	229	700
■	= gray	401	413
•	= French Knots: gray		
|	= Backstitch: gray		

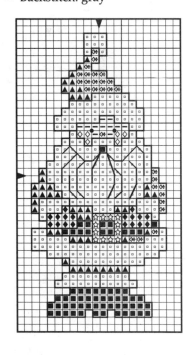

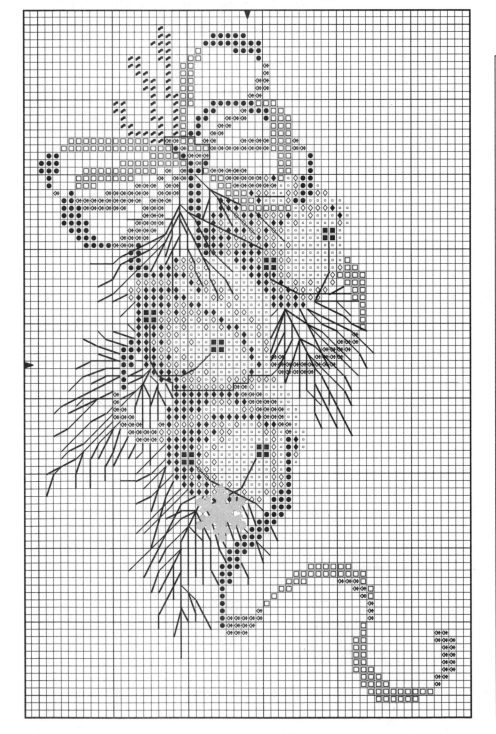

343 Drummer's Delight
(41 wide x 32 high)

		Anchor	DMC
●	= red	47	321
○	= yellow	301	744
⊞	= lt gold	305	743
■	= med gold	307	783
△	= very lt green	842	3013
+	= lt green	843	3012
	med green	861	520
★	= dk green	217	561
◆	= blue	131	799
▫	= tan	885	739
	rust	351	400
\	= Straight Stitches: rust		
		= Backstitch: med green		

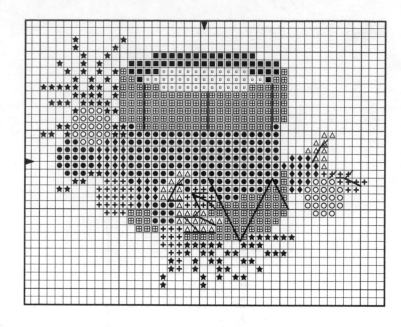

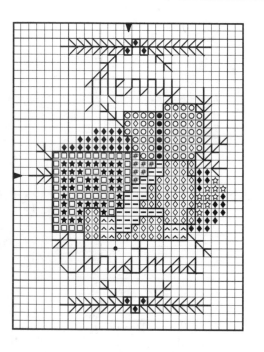

344 Christmas Toys
(25 wide x 34 high)

		Anchor	DMC
−	= white	2	blanc
◇	= pink	74	3354
◆	= red	19	304
∧	= peach	366	951
☆	= gold	891	676
#	= green	258	904
○	= lt blue	920	932
●	= dk blue	921	931
□	= lt brown	363	436
★	= med brown	371	433
•	= French Knot: red		
		= Backstitch:		
	"Merry Christmas," berries—red		
	branches—green		
	doll, block—med brown		

345 Partridge In Pear Tree
(25 wide x 23 high)

		Anchor	DMC
▫	= lt pink	50	605
✳	= dk pink	76	961
◇	= yellow	305	743
	green	258	905
▽	= lt blue	130	809
★	= dk blue	132	797
+	= purple	110	208
▲	= brown	357	433
•	= French Knots: dk pink		
		= Backstitch:		
	scroll—green		
	head & tail feathers—purple		
	remaining partridge—brown		

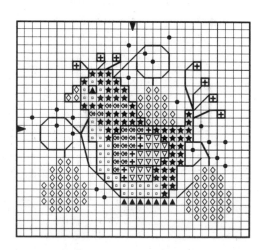

346 **Panda Surprise**
(48 wide x 23 high)

		Anchor	DMC
▫	= white	2	blanc
✤	= pink	24	963
■	= black	403	310
		= Backstitch: black	

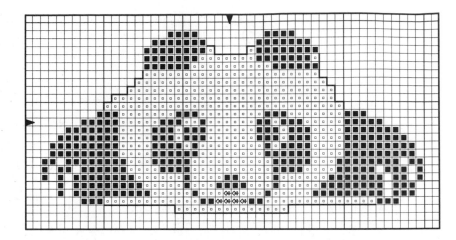

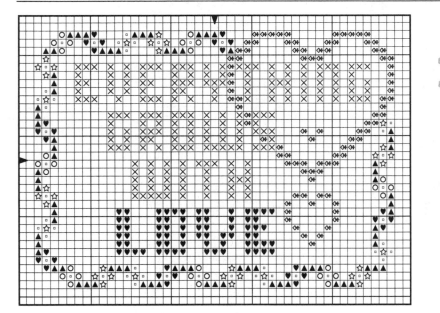

347 **Everything Grows With Love**
(45 wide x 32 high)

		Anchor	DMC
✕	= lt rose	25	3326
✤	= med rose	27	899
♥	= dk rose	42	326
☆	= peach	8	3824
▫	= yellow	305	743
▲	= green	246	986
○	= blue	161	813

348 **Mistletoe Magic** (74 wide x 29 high)

		Anchor	DMC			Anchor	DMC
⊙	= cream	387	712	▲ = med green		243	703
✤	= pink	50	605	dk green		217	561
△	= lt green	240	368	| = Backstitch: dk green			

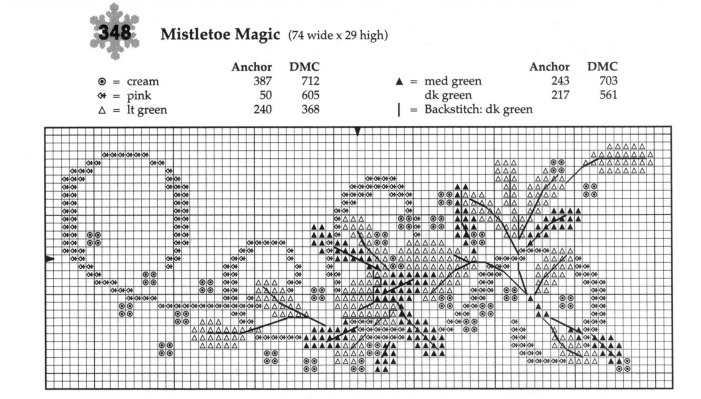

349 Happy Cat
(28 wide x 34 high)

			Anchor	DMC
▫	=	cream	926	712
✕	=	lt pink	893	224
★	=	dk pink	896	3721
✕	=	peach	882	758
✿	=	green	243	703
♥	=	rust	5975	356
■	=	black	403	310
		=	Backstitch: dk pink		

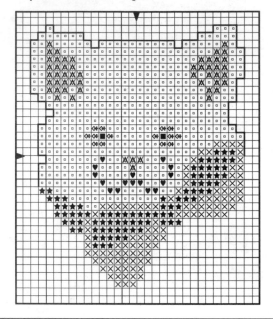

350 Baby Love
(27 wide x 22 high)

			Anchor	DMC
✕	=	pink	74	3354
▫	=	yellow	295	726
−	=	green	209	913
◉	=	blue	160	827
✿	=	fuchsia	87	3607

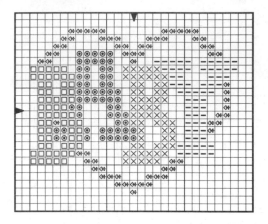

351 Holiday Angel
(42 wide x 27 high)

			Anchor	DMC
●	=	red	35	3801
▫	=	peach	778	754
◇	=	gold	307	783
✕	=	lt green	266	3347
■	=	dk green	268	469
☆	=	blue	168	3810
+	=	brown	351	400
		=	Backstitch: brown		

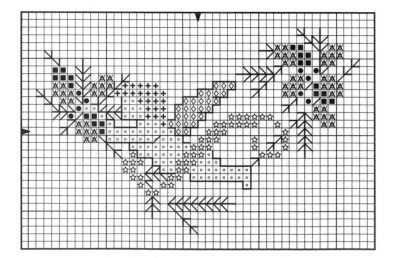

352 May Our Home Be Warm
(26 wide x 26 high)

			Anchor	DMC
○	=	med pink	66	3688
★	=	dk pink	42	309
◆	=	green	242	989
		blue	146	798
		brown	357	433
◌	=	Lazy Daisies:		

bottom outer & top flowers—med pink
bottom center flowers—blue
• = French Knots: med pink
| | = Backstitch:
  "May" —med pink
  "Warm"—dk pink
  stems—green
  "Home"—blue
  "Our," "be"—brown

353 Happy New Home
(25 wide x 25 high)

		Anchor	DMC
□ =	lt rose	74	3354
★ =	dk rose	69	3687
◉ =	yellow	301	744
	lt green	266	3347
◆ =	dk green	268	469
	brown	380	838
• =	French Knots: lt green		
	=	Backstitch: stems—dk green	lettering—brown	

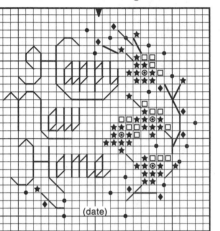

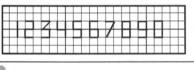

354 Little Rocking Horse
(25 wide x 26 high)

		Anchor	DMC
▫ =	white	2	blanc
☆ =	pink	27	899
+ =	red	59	326
◇ =	yellow	297	973
◆ =	green	923	699
□ =	lt blue	160	827
▼ =	dk blue	169	517
■ =	brown	360	898
• =	French Knots: red		
	=	Backstitch: bridle—yellow		
	branches—green	stirrup—brown	

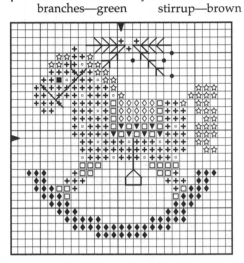

355 Singing Angel
(24 wide x 27 high)

		Anchor	DMC
− =	white	2	blanc
△ =	lt pink	73	963
+ =	med pink	76	961
◆ =	rose	59	600
▫ =	peach	778	754
☆ =	gold	306	725
▼ =	brown	371	433
• =	French Knot: rose		
	=	Backstitch: wings—med pink		
	sleeves, hands, eyes—brown		

356 Choo-Choo Train
(44 wide x 20 high)

		Anchor	DMC
▫ =	white	2	blanc
✤ =	lt pink	50	957
◉ =	med pink	40	956
● =	dk pink	59	326
○ =	lt orange	323	722
# =	med orange	329	3340
◇ =	yellow	295	726
∿ =	gold	307	783
− =	lt green	203	954
△ =	med green	205	912
★ =	dk green	229	910
■ =	gray	236	3799
	=	Backstitch: gray		

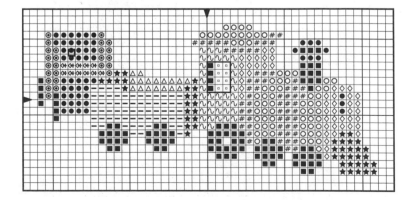

147

357 Trumpeting Angel
(42 wide x 26 high)

			Anchor	DMC
□	=	white	2	blanc
✿	=	lt pink	74	3354
♥	=	dk pink	78	3685
~	=	peach	778	3774
◇	=	lt yellow	301	744
♦	=	dk yellow	302	743
★	=	gold	306	783
∧	=	lt turquoise	185	964
●	=	dk turquoise	188	3812
⊕	=	rust	365	435
⊠	=	lt gray	234	762
■	=	dk gray	401	413
		=	Backstitch: lt pink		

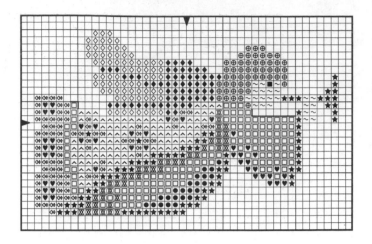

358 Holiday Music
(76 wide x 81 high)

			Anchor	DMC
○	=	med pink	27	899
♦	=	dk pink	42	309
●	=	red	20	498
☆	=	yellow	305	743
+	=	gold	308	782
−	=	yellow-green	256	704
		lt green	215	320
◉	=	med green	217	367
★	=	dk green	246	986
✿	=	blue	161	826
□	=	tan	362	437
■	=	brown	371	433
＼	=	Straight Stitch: brown		
		=	Backstitch: lt green		

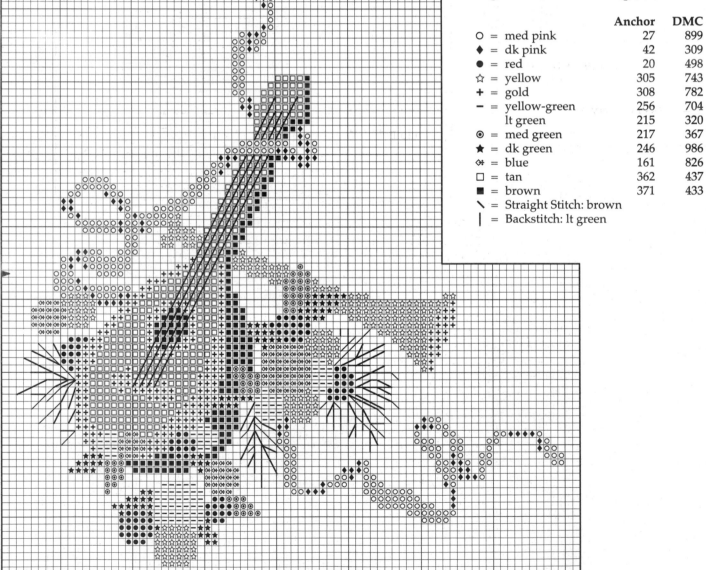

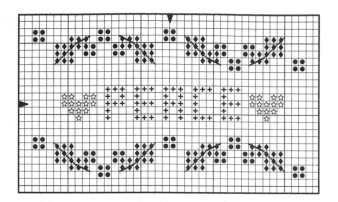

359 Winter Peace
(38 wide x 21 high)

		Anchor	DMC
☆ =	med red	1024	3328
● =	dk red	47	321
◆ =	med green	217	367
	dk green	246	986

Kreinik #8 Braid

+ =	gold		028

| = Backstitch: dk green

360 Poinsettia Glow
(96 wide x 92 high)

		Anchor	DMC
▫ =	lt pink	24	776
△ =	med pink	27	899
+ =	med red	42	309
⋈ =	dk red	20	498
● =	very dk red	44	814
★ =	gold	306	725
◇ =	lt green	215	320
▣ =	med green	217	367

Kreinik #8 Braid

O =	gold		002HL

| = Backstitch: very dk red

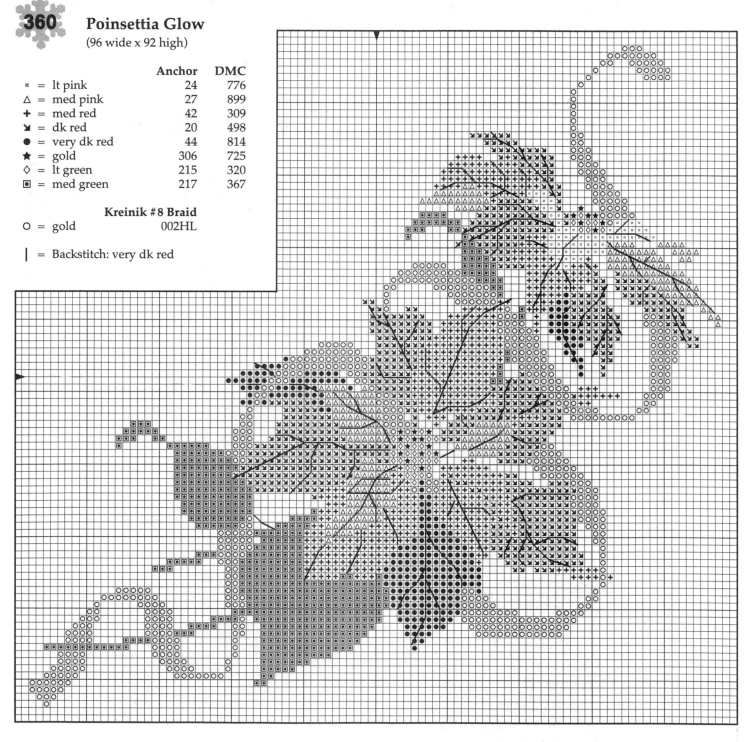

361 **The Bell Of Noel**
(34 wide x 39 high)

		Anchor	DMC
◇ =	med red	35	3801
★ =	dk red	47	304
▼ =	green	229	700
• =	French Knots: green		
| =	Backstitch:		
	bell outline—dk red		
	leaves—green		

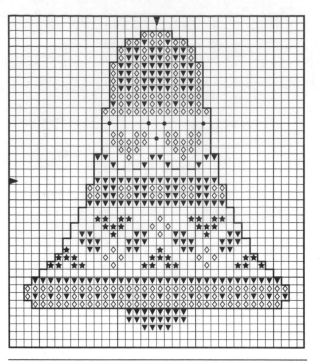

362 **Pair Of Angels**
(88 wide x 46 high)

		Anchor	DMC			Anchor	DMC
★ =	pink	52	957	+ =	dk green	245	986
⌁ =	lt red	41	335	◇ =	lt blue	117	341
	med red	42	309	◆ =	med blue	118	340
	dk red	78	3685	△ =	lt purple	95	554
▫ =	peach	868	353	▲ =	med purple	97	553
✴ =	orange	328	3341	⌐ =	brown	352	300
~ =	lt yellow	295	726	• =	French Knots: med red		
– =	med yellow	306	725	| =	Backstitch:		
O =	lt gold	891	676		ribbon—dk red		
◉ =	dk gold	901	680		stems—dk green		
× =	lt green	240	368		eyes—brown (2 strands)		

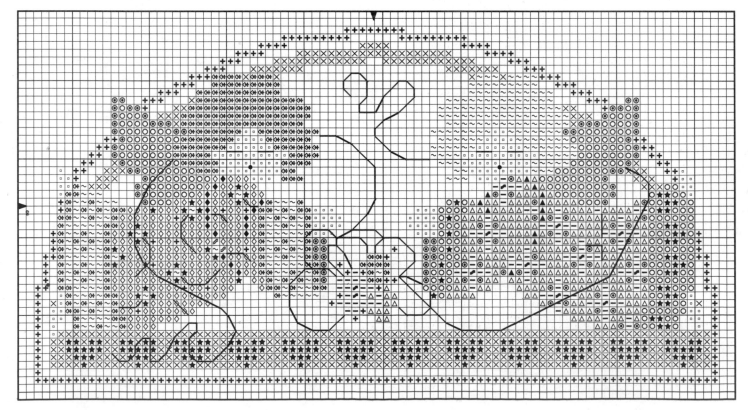

363 Bird On The Holly Perch

(47 wide x 34 high)

		Anchor	DMC
− =	white	2	blanc
+ =	red	19	304
☆ =	peach	35	3705
▫ =	lt orange	347	402
◆ =	dk orange	324	922
▽ =	lt green	238	703
▲ =	med green	227	701
	dk green	268	469
□ =	lt blue	920	932
● =	dk blue	921	931
■ =	brown	357	433
★ =	gray	844	3012

| = Backstitch:
beak—dk orange
leaves, pine—dk green
branches—brown
berries, bird's eye, outline, &
    feathers—gray

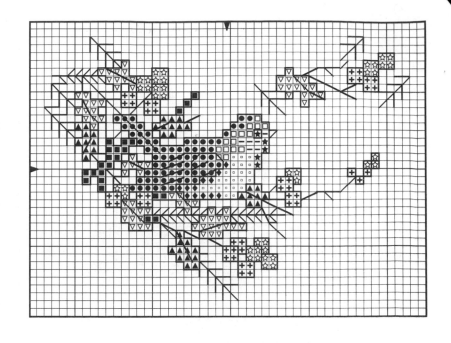

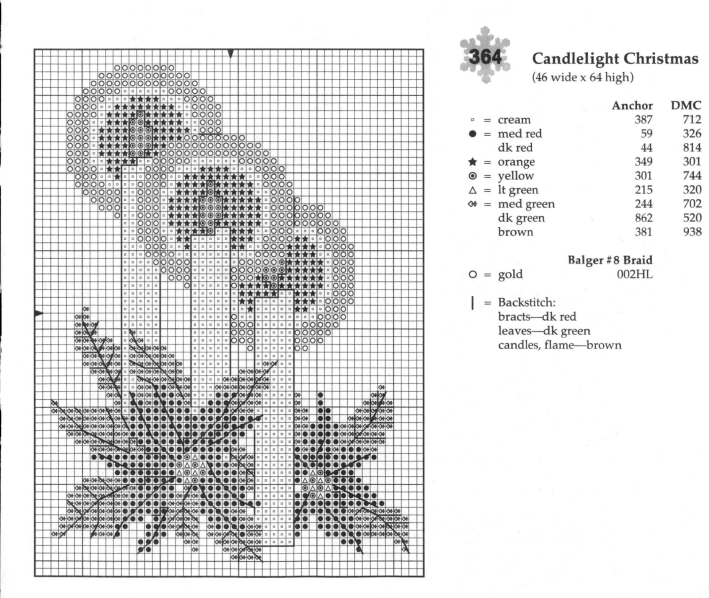

364 Candlelight Christmas

(46 wide x 64 high)

		Anchor	DMC
▫ =	cream	387	712
● =	med red	59	326
	dk red	44	814
★ =	orange	349	301
◉ =	yellow	301	744
△ =	lt green	215	320
❖ =	med green	244	702
	dk green	862	520
	brown	381	938

Balger #8 Braid

O =	gold		002HL

| = Backstitch:
bracts—dk red
leaves—dk green
candles, flame—brown

365 **Alphabet**

Kreinik #8 Braid
O = gold   002HL

	Anchor	DMC
red	19	304
♦ = green	246	986

• = French Knots: red
| = Backstitch: green

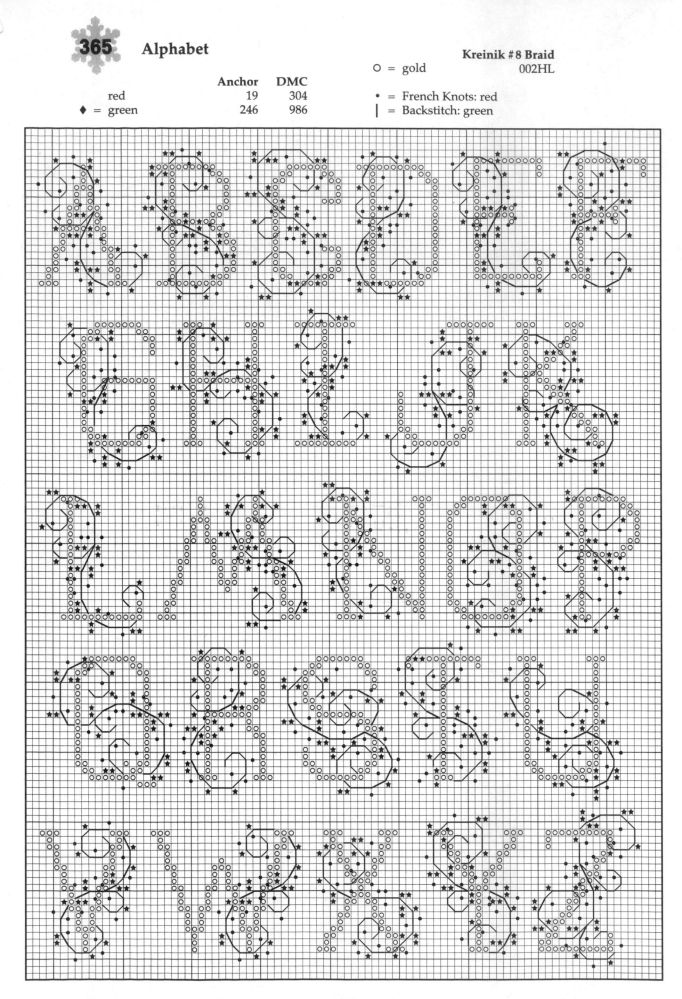